611

CR

D0859550

RECYCLE

TEAM GREEN SCIENCE PROJECTS

GREEN
SCIENCE
PROJECTS
FOR A
SUSTAINABLE
PLANET

Robert Gardner

E **Enslow Publishers, Inc.**
40 Industrial Road
Box 398
Berkeley Heights, NJ 07922
USA
http://www.enslow.com

RECYCLE
GREEN Science Projects for a Sustainable PLANET

Library of Congress Cataloging-in-Publication Data

Gardner, Robert, 1929–
    Recycle : green science projects for a sustainable planet / Robert Gardner.
       p. cm. — (Team green science projects)
    Includes bibliographical references and index.
    Summary: "Provides environmentally friendly 'green' science projects about recycling"—
       Provided by publisher.
    ISBN 978-0-7660-3648-2
    1. Recycling (Waste, etc.)—Juvenile literature. 2. Recycling (Waste, etc.)—Environmental
       aspects—Juvenile literature. I. Title.
    TD794.5.G37 2011
    628.4'458—dc22
                               2009037903

Printed in the United States of America

092010 Lake Book Manufacturing, Inc., Melrose Park, IL

10 9 8 7 6 5 4 3 2 1

To Our Readers: We have done our best to make sure all Internet Addresses in this book were active and appropriate when we went to press. However, the author and the publisher have no control over and assume no liability for the material available on those Internet sites or on other Web sites they may link to. Any comments or suggestions can be sent by e-mail to comments@enslow.com or to the address on the back cover.

♻ Enslow Publishers, Inc., is committed to printing our books on recycled paper. The paper in every book contains 10% to 30% post-consumer waste (PCW). The cover board on the outside of each book contains 100% PCW. Our goal is to do our part to help young people and the environment too!

Illustration Credits: Shutterstock.com, pp. 18, 122; Stephen Rountree (www.rountreegraphics.com), pp. 30, 39, 55, 58, 68, 82, 101, 107, 111; Tom LaBaff, pp. 36, 64, 84; Tom LaBaff and Stephanie LaBaff, pp. 13, 23.

Photo Credits: All photos by Shutterstock.com, except © Jani Bryson/iStockphoto.com, p. 2; © John Krajewski/iStockphoto.com, p. 73; © Jörg Riethausen/iStockphoto.com, p. 75; © Mark Wragg/iStockphoto.com, p. 6; © Ryan Lane/iStockphoto.com, p. 114.

Cover Photo: Shutterstock.com

Contents

Introduction 7

    The Scientific Method 8

    Science Fairs 10

    Safety First 11

Chapter 1

Plastics and Recycling 12

  1.1 **Polymers and Diapers (An Experiment)** 15

  1.2 **Numbered Plastics (An Activity)** 20

  1.3 **Liquids, Solids, Density, and Sink or Float (A Demonstration)** 21

  1.4 **Identifying Plastics by Their Densities (An Experiment)** 25

  1.5 **Do Plastics Burn? (An Experiment)** 29

Chapter 2

Solid Waste and Decomposition 32

  2.1 **Landfill Pollution (A Model)** 35

  2.2 **Build a Better Landfill (A Model)** 38

  2.3 **Decomposers in Soil (An Experiment)** 41

  2.4 **Watching Things Decay (An Observation)** 44

  2.5 **Water and Decay (An Experiment)** 45

  2.6 **What Redi Discovered (An Experiment)** 47

 Indicates experiments that offer ideas for science fair projects.

Chapter 3

The Greening of Waste 50

☑ 3.1   Waste to Energy: An Electric Generator
(A Demonstration) 53

3.2   Composting (An Activity) 57

3.3   Composting with Earthworms (An Activity) 61

3.4   Surface Area and Volume (A Demonstration) 63

3.5   Polluting Substances Measured in Parts
Per Million (An Activity) 65

Chapter 4

More Things to Recycle 74

☑ 4.1   Separating Aluminum and Steel "Cans"
(An Experiment) 80

☑ 4.2   Separating Aluminum and Steel "Cans"
(A Demonstration) 83

4.3   Viewing Paper Fibers (An Observation) 91

☑ 4.4   Recycling Paper (A Demonstration) 92

4.5   Separating Trash for Recycling (An Experiment) 95

4.6   Natural Resources Trapped in Solid Waste
(An Activity) 97

Chapter 5

What Can YOU Do? 99

5.1   Organize a Litter Removal Squad (An Activity) 100

5.2   Beachcombing for Litter (An Activity) 103

5.3   Simulating Entanglement (A Demonstration) 106

☑ 5.4   Precycling: Consider the Packaging Before
You Buy (An Analysis) 109

 Indicates experiments that offer ideas for science fair projects.

5.5   **Find Out About Recycling in Your Town or City (An Activity)** 115

5.6   **Recycling at School (An Activity)** 116

5.7   **Recycling in the Classroom (An Experiment)** 118

5.8   **A Zero-Waste Lunch (An Activity)** 120

5.9   **Which Cup Should I Buy for One-Time Use? (An Experiment)** 121

Glossary 123

Appendix: Science Supply Companies 125

Further Reading and Internet Addresses 126

Index 127

top 5 ways to use this bag

MADE OF 100% RECYCLED PAPER

Introduction

There's an old saying that we hear more often as people adopt a "green" lifestyle: "Use it up, wear it out, make it do, or do without." Things we can reuse include glass and plastic bottles, aluminum and steel cans, paper, cardboard, various plastic containers, ink cartridges, and many other items. Some may be used again and again if we recycle them. We can also find new uses for things we might otherwise throw away. A worn-out shower curtain can serve as a painter's drop cloth, an empty plastic butter tub can hold leftover food in the refrigerator, worn-out socks and shirts can be used as dust cloths or to clean up spills, and so on.

In this book, you will learn about recycling and how it can save energy as well as valuable resources that are growing ever more scarce. By doing experiments, you will gain a better understanding of why recycling is important and why it plays a role in creating a greener world.

At times, as you carry out the experiments, demonstrations, and various activities in this book, you may need a partner to help you. It would be best to work with someone who enjoys experimenting as much as you do. That way, you will both have fun with them. **If any safety issue or danger is involved in doing an experiment, you will be warned. In some cases, to avoid danger, you will be asked to work with an adult. Please do so.** Don't take any chances that could lead to an injury.

Like any good scientist, you will find it useful to record your ideas, notes, data, and anything you can conclude from your investigations in a notebook. By doing so, you can keep track of the information you gather and the conclusions you reach. It will allow you to refer to things you have done and help you do future projects.

The Scientific Method

Scientists look at the world and try to understand how things work. They conduct research and make careful observations. Different areas of science use different approaches. Depending on the problem, one method is likely to be better than another. Designing a new medicine for heart disease, studying the spread of an invasive plant such as purple loosestrife, and finding evidence of water on Mars require different methods.

Despite the differences, all scientists use a similar general approach in doing experiments. It is called the scientific method. In most experiments, some or all of the following steps are used: making an observation, formulating a question, making a hypothesis (a possible answer to the question) and a prediction (an if-then statement), designing and conducting an experiment to test the hypothesis, analyzing results and drawing conclusions about your prediction, and accepting or rejecting the hypothesis. Scientists then share their findings by writing articles that are published in journals.

You might wonder how to start an experiment. When you observe something in the world, you may become curious and ask a question. Your question, which could arise from an earlier experiment or from reading, may be answered by a well-designed investigation. Once you have a question, you can make a hypothesis. Your hypothesis is a possible answer to the question (what you think will happen). Then you can design an experiment to test your hypothesis.

In most cases, it is appropriate to do a controlled experiment. This means having two groups that are treated exactly the same except for the single factor being tested. That factor is often called a variable.

For example, suppose your question is "How do the densities of aluminum and steel cans compare?" Your hypothesis might be that steel cans are denser than aluminum cans. You could weigh the cans. A large measuring cup could be used to measure the volume of the cans by water displacement. During the experiment, you would collect data. You would measure and record the mass and volume of each type of can. You would then divide the masses by their volumes. By comparing the results, you would draw a conclusion. The procedure is the same for both cans—the variable is the makeup of the cans.

Two other terms are often used in scientific experiments—*dependent* and *independent variables*. The dependent variable here is density. It depends on the mass and volumes of the cans. The independent variables are their volumes and masses. After the data is collected, it is analyzed to see if it supports or rejects the hypothesis. The results of one experiment often lead you to related questions. Or they may send you off in a different direction. Whatever the results, something can be learned from every experiment.

Science Fairs

Some of the activities in this book contain ideas you might use at a science fair. Those projects are indicated with a symbol (✅). However, judges at science fairs do not reward projects or experiments that are simply copied from a book. If you decide to use an experiment or idea found in this book for a science fair, find ways to modify or extend it. This should not be difficult. As you carry out investigations, new ideas will come to mind. You will think of questions that experiments can answer. The experiments will make excellent science fair projects, particularly because the ideas are your own and are interesting to you.

Science fair judges tend to reward creative thought and imagination. For example, a diagram or model of a recycling center would not impress most judges; however, a unique way to separate a mix of recyclable items would be likely to attract their attention. It is difficult to be creative or imaginative unless you are really interested in your project. Therefore, try to choose an investigation that excites you. And before you jump into a project, consider, too, your own talents and the cost of the materials you will need.

If you decide to enter a science fair and have never done so, read some of the books listed in the Further Reading section. Some of these books deal specifically with science fairs. They provide plenty of helpful hints and useful information. The books will help you avoid the pitfalls that sometimes plague first-time entrants. You will learn how to prepare appealing reports that include charts and graphs, how to set up and display your work, how to present your project, and how to relate to judges and visitors.

Safety First

As with many activities, safety is important in science. Certain rules apply when doing experiments. Some of the rules below may seem obvious to you, others may not, but it is important that you follow all of them.

1. Have **an adult** help you whenever the book advises.

2. Wear eye protection and closed-toe shoes (not sandals). Tie back long hair.

3. Do not eat or drink while experimenting. Never taste substances being used (unless instructed to do so).

4. Do not touch chemicals.

5. The liquid in some thermometers is mercury (a dense liquid metal). It is dangerous to touch mercury or breathe mercury vapor, and such thermometers have been banned in many states. When doing these experiments, use only non-mercury thermometers, such as those filled with alcohol. If you have a mercury thermometer in the house, **ask an adult** if it can be taken to a local thermometer exchange location.

6. Do only those experiments that are described in the book or those that have been approved by **an adult**.

7. Maintain a serious attitude while conducting experiments. Never engage in horseplay or play practical jokes.

8. Before beginning an experiment, read all the instructions carefully and be sure you understand them.

9. Remove all items not needed for the experiment from your work space.

10. At the end of every activity, clean all materials used and put them away. Then wash your hands thoroughly with soap and water.

Plastics and Recycling

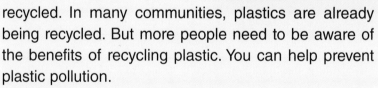

Earth has become polluted with plastics, both on land and sea. But this pollution need not increase. Plastics can be recycled. In many communities, plastics are already being recycled. But more people need to be aware of the benefits of recycling plastic. You can help prevent plastic pollution.

Plastics are made from organic compounds, which are substances that contain carbon. Carbon compounds were originally called organic because they come from organisms—living things. It was believed that only plants and animals could make organic compounds. Then in 1828, a German chemist, Freidrich Wohler (1800–1882), showed that organic compounds can be prepared in a laboratory. He made urea from ammonium cyanate. Urea is an organic compound in urine. But ammonium cyanate is not made by living organisms.

More recently, chemists have been able to join organic molecules found in crude oil to form huge, long, chainlike molecules. The joining of like molecules to form heavier ones is called *polymerization* [pah lih mer ih ZAY shun]. These large molecules are called polymers. The prefix *poly*, which means "many," indicates that they are made by combining many molecules. Figure 1a shows how two ethylene (ethene)

Figure 1

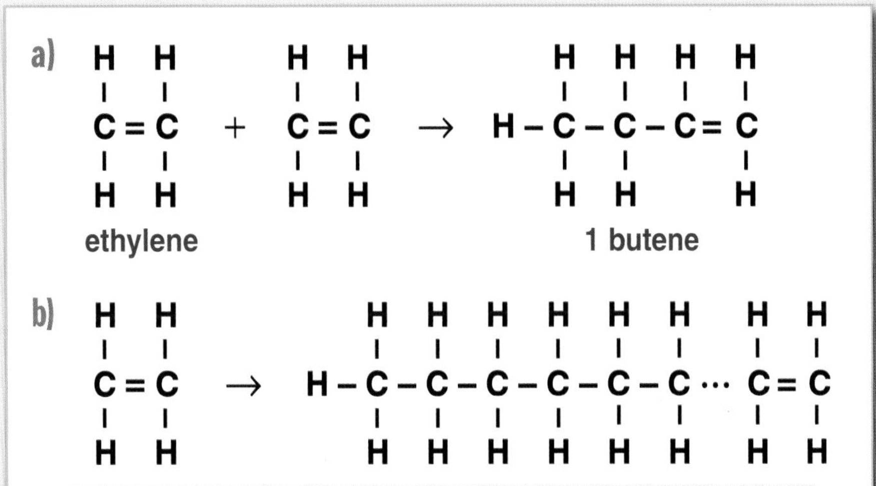

a)
```
  H   H          H   H                 H   H   H   H
  |   |          |   |                 |   |   |   |
  C = C    +     C = C      →      H – C – C – C = C
  |   |          |   |                 |   |       |
  H   H          H   H                 H   H       H
ethylene                                   1 butene
```

b)
```
  H   H                    H   H   H   H   H   H      H   H
  |   |                    |   |   |   |   |   |      |   |
  C = C      →      H – C – C – C – C – C – C ··· C = C
  |   |                    |   |   |   |   |   |      |   |
  H   H                    H   H   H   H   H   H      H   H
```

1. a) Two molecules of ethylene (C_2H_4) join to form a molecule of butene (C_4H_8). The dashes represent chemical bonds (shared electrons) joining carbon and hydrogen atoms in the molecule.
   b) Many ethylene molecules can join to form very large molecules called polymers.

molecules can join to form a molecule of butene. Figure 1b shows you that many ethylene molecules can join to form a long chainlike hydrocarbon (a compound that contains only hydrogen and carbon) called a polymer.

There are many natural polymers such as starch, cellulose, fats, waxes, oils, and proteins. Proteins include enzymes, hormones, wool, and silk. Synthetic (human-made) polymers are found in plastics and textiles such as Plexiglas®, nylon, and polyester.

Plastic products are in wide use. Some things made of plastic include cell phones, toys, credit cards, computers, TVs, CDs, DVDs, radios, clocks, contact lenses, artificial hips and knees, heart valves, disposable coffee cups, and food containers, to name a few. On the plus side, items made of plastics are lightweight, inexpensive, durable, and convenient. However, they are made from petroleum, a nonrenewable resource (one that cannot be replaced). Many plastics are not recycled. Because they are not biodegradable (capable of being decomposed by bacteria), they add indestructible bulk to landfills.

Search your home for things made of plastic. They should be easy to find. How many can you identify? If you don't know whether an item is made of plastic, **ask an adult**.

1.1 Polymers and Diapers
(An Experiment)

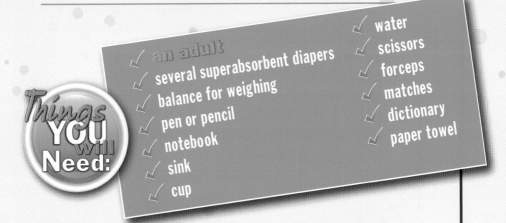

Things YOU will Need:

- an adult
- several superabsorbent diapers
- balance for weighing
- pen or pencil
- notebook
- sink
- cup
- water
- scissors
- forceps
- matches
- dictionary
- paper towel

Sodium polyacrylate, a synthetic polymer, is found in superabsorbent diapers. Why do you think this polymer is found in diapers? Form a hypothesis. Then do this experiment.

1. Remove a superabsorbent diaper from a package. Weigh it (in grams) and record its weight.

2. Put the diaper in a sink and open it. The polymer is enclosed by a thin rectangular cloth that runs along the center of the diaper.

3. Carefully pour a cup of water along the length of the central part of the diaper. What happens to the water?

4. Continue to add water until the diaper will absorb no more.

5. Lift the diaper and let any excess water drain into the sink. Now reweigh the diaper. Record the new weight. How much water was absorbed?

6. How much water was absorbed by one gram of the polymer? To find out, use scissors to carefully cut away the portion of a dry diaper that contains the polymer. Weigh and record the polymer's weight.

7. To find the ratio of the weight of water absorbed per gram of polymer, divide the weight of the water absorbed by the weight of the polymer.

$$\text{ratio of water weight absorbed per gram of polymer} = \frac{\text{weight of water absorbed (g)}}{\text{weight of polymer (g)}}$$

8. To see what the polymer in a dry diaper looks like, use scissors to cut through the thin cloth that covers the sodium polyacrylate. What does the polymer look like? Describe its texture.

9. Will it burn? To find out, use forceps to hold a sample of the polymer over a sink. **Ask an adult** to try to ignite the polymer with a match. Is the polymer flammable? What evidence do you have that polyacrylate is an organic compound? Remember that organic molecules contain carbon. Why are there warnings on diaper packages telling people not to allow diapered babies near flames?

10. To see what the wet polymer looks like, make a small slit in the diaper saturated with water. Describe the polymer after it has absorbed water.

11. Look up the words *hydrophilic* and *hydrophobic*. Is sodium polyacrylate hydrophilic or hydrophobic?

Do you think there should be warnings on superabsorbent diapers telling parents not to let babies wear such a diaper in a swimming pool?

12. Put a small sample of the wet polymer on a paper towel. Place the towel in a warm (not hot) place. Does the wet polymer eventually dry? Does it return to its original form? If it does, will it still absorb water?

Recycling and Plastics

During World War II, many materials were scarce because they were used for the war effort. Paper, glass, metals, even cooking fat were recycled. More recently, recycling has increased again as people realize that it contributes to a greener world.

Recycling is a way to conserve energy. Making a new aluminum can from recycled metal requires only 5 percent of the energy needed to make the same can from bauxite ore, a major source of aluminum. The energy conserved by recycling paper, glass, and steel is less dramatic. However, recycling significantly reduces the energy required to produce these items from raw materials.

Recycling plastics is complicated because there are so many types. The seven most common types are labeled for recycling purposes. On the bottom and lids of most plastic containers you will find an imprinted triangle. Inside the triangle you will see a number, as shown in Figure 2. In some cities and towns, only plastics labeled 1 or 2 are recycled.

A triangle with a 1 in its center indicates that the plastic is made of PETE (or PET). PETE stands for the polymer *polyethylene terephthalate* (pa lee ETH uh leen teh ruh THAL ayt). PETE is commonly used to make soda bottles because it does not allow carbon dioxide bubbles to escape. When recycled, this polymer can be melted and drawn into long fibers.

Figure 2

The symbols used to identify the seven common types of plastic. These symbols can help people determine what can be recycled in their town.

The fibers are used to make carpets and fabric for clothing and shopping bags.

Number 2 plastic (HDPE), high-density polyethylene, can be either clear or colored. It is used to make milk and water jugs, soap bottles, pails, and some toys. Because it is very strong, it can be recycled into plastic lumber, fence posts, benches, and even bullet-proof vests for soldiers and police officers.

Number 3 (V or PVC) is polyvinyl chloride. It is used in making clear food packaging, plumbing pipes, bottles for cooking oil, shrink wrap, automobile dash-boards, and seat covers. It can be recycled into floor mats, pipes, hoses, and mud flaps.

Number 4 (LDPE), low-density polyethylene, is a very light and flexible plastic that is used to make bags that enclose food products. It is also used as covers for some plastic containers.

Number 2 and 4 plastics are both polymers of the same molecule—polyethylene. However, the number 2 molecules are long chains of polyethylene that pack closely together, making a dense plastic. The method used in making number 4 plastic causes the molecules to branch. The branches keep the molecules from fitting closely together. As a result, this plastic has a lower density than number 2.

Number 5 (PP) is polypropylene (pah lee PROH puh leen). It is moisture-resistant, flexible, and does not deform when filled with hot liquids. Medicine vials, bottle caps, and yogurt, margarine, and other food containers are commonly made from this plastic.

Number 6 (PS) is polystyrene (pah lee STY reen). It is used to make foam coffee cups, cutlery, meat trays, foam insulation, packing peanuts, and CD covers. These plastic products are very light because they are mostly air.

Number 7 (OTHER) is made from a mixture of any of the other plastics. It is seldom recycled because of the expense involved in separating its components.

The number associated with each type of plastic is also the number used to code the plastic for recycling purposes. Many communities ask citizens to recycle plastics. The code is useful in identifying the type of plastic that the city or town will accept for recycling.

1.2 **Numbered Plastics**

(An Activity)

1. Look for the numbers inside the little triangles on the bottoms of a variety of plastic articles. Look for plastics numbered 1 through 7.

2. Try to find at least one of each kind. Number 1 (PET) and 2 (HDPE) plastics are easy to find and are the two most commonly recycled. Yogurt containers are commonly made of number 5 (PP), and foam coffee cups and tape dispensers are a common source of number 6 (PS).

3. Look for the other numbered plastics and collect as many as you can. If some of the plastic containers are still partially filled, ask permission to place their contents in another container or wait until they are empty.

4. Wash and dry the numbered plastics you find and save them for Experiment 1.4.

1.3 Liquids, Solids, Density, and Sink or Float

(A Demonstration)

Things YOU will Need:

- water
- balance for weighing
- 100-mL graduated cylinder
- pen or pencil
- notebook
- rubbing alcohol
- cooking oil
- soap
- block of wood
- metric ruler
- deep pan
- steel washers, nuts, or bolts

In Experiment 1.4 you will need to understand density and how density affects whether a solid plastic sinks or floats in a liquid. This demonstration will provide what you need to know about finding density.

The density of a substance is its mass per volume. That is,

$$\text{density} = \frac{\text{mass}}{\text{volume}}, \text{ or } D = \frac{M}{V}$$

For liquids, density is usually measured in grams per milliliter (g/mL). Which do you predict is more dense, water or cooking oil?

1. To find the density of water, weigh a 100-mL graduated cylinder. (Actually, a graduated cylinder of any size will do.) Record its mass in grams.

2. Fill the cylinder to the 100-mL line with water. Be sure the bottom of the curved surface of the water (meniscus) just touches the 100-mL line (Figure 3).

3. Reweigh the water-filled cylinder. Record the mass of the water and graduated cylinder. How can you find the weight of the water alone?

   What is the mass in grams of 100 mL of water? What is the density of water in grams per milliliter (g/mL)?

4. Dry the graduated cylinder.

5. Repeat the experiment using rubbing alcohol. What is the density of rubbing alcohol?

6. Dry the graduated cylinder.

   Which do you predict is more dense, rubbing alcohol or cooking oil?

7. To check your prediction, repeat the experiment using cooking oil. What is the density of cooking oil? Is it more or less dense than rubbing alcohol? Was your prediction correct?

8. Wash the graduated cylinder thoroughly with soap and water.

9. Find the density of a block of wood. First, measure and record its length, width, and height. Use these measurements to find its volume in cubic centimeters (cm^3). (A cubic centimeter [cm^3] and a milliliter [mL] are equal in volume.

Figure 3

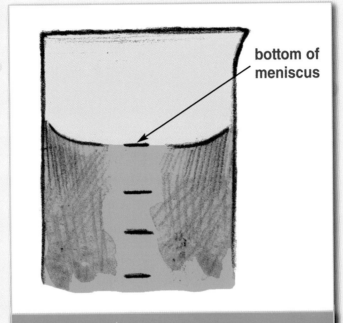

bottom of meniscus

Fill a graduated cylinder to the 100-mL line with water. The surface of the water is curved because water adheres (sticks) to glass or plastic. The curved surface is called a meniscus. The bottom of the meniscus should touch the line used to measure volume.

Milliliters are commonly used to measure the volume of liquids and gases; cubic centimeters are used to measure the volume of solids.)

10. Weigh the block and record its mass. Then calculate the block's density in grams per cubic centimeter (g/cm^3).

Compare the density of the wood with the density of water, which you probably found to be about one gram per milliliter (1 g/mL). Do you think the wood will sink or float in water?

11. Put the wood block in a pan filled with water. Does it sink or float? Were you right?

12. Next, find the density of some steel objects such as washers, nuts, or bolts. Gather a number of them and weigh them.

13. Carefully drop the objects into a 100-mL graduated cylinder that holds 50 mL of water. If the water rises to the 85-mL line, you know the volume of the washers is 35 mL (85 mL–50 mL). Would you expect the steel to be more or less dense than water?

14. Calculate the density of the steel. Were you right?

15. If you add cooking oil to water, would you expect it to sink or float? Try it. Were you right?

Idea for a Science Fair Project

Compare the densities of different metals such as aluminum (Al), magnesium (Mg), iron (Fe), copper (Cu), lead (Pb), tin (Sn), and zinc (Zn). Do their relative densities correspond to their relative atomic weights as found on the periodic table of elements?

1.4 Identifying Plastics by Their Densities
(An Experiment)

The densities of some plastics are quite close in value, so how do you think different plastics can be identified by their densities? Form a hypothesis. Then do this experiment.

As you read, plastics are formed by the polymerization of organic compounds. Several common plastics are used to package foods and liquids. These numbered plastics include (1) polyethylene terephthalate (PET),

(2) high-density polyethylene (HDPE), (3) polyvinyl chloride (PVC), (4) low-density polyethylene (LDPE), (5) polypropylene (PP), (6) polystyrene (PS), and (7) OTHER.

To carry out this experiment, obtain one sample for each of the seven numbered plastics, or as many of the seven as possible.

1. Use scissors or shears to cut at least seven small pieces from each kind of plastic. The samples can be squares roughly 2 cm (1 in) on a side. Keep the plastic samples separated by number. Put each kind of plastic in a labeled envelope or container.

2. Can you identify these plastics by such properties as their appearance, color, flexibility, response to bending, or texture?

One very useful property in identifying substances is their density. You found the densities of water, cooking oil, rubbing alcohol, wood, and steel in Experiment 1.3. You also found that solids float in liquids that are denser than the solid. A solid will sink if it is more dense than the liquid in which it is placed.

It would be difficult to find the density of the different samples of plastic you have collected. You might weigh the small pieces and put them in a graduated cylinder to see how much water they displace. However, it would be difficult to submerge them in the cylinder if they float. Furthermore, their volumes would be too small to measure accurately.

There is another way to find their approximate densities. You can place them in liquids whose density you know and see whether they sink or float. For example, if the pieces of a numbered plastic float in water, you know

If you did Experiment 1.3, you already know the density of water, cooking oil, and rubbing alcohol. You can also prepare some other liquids whose densities will be different from those of the three liquids you have already measured.

3. Prepare each of the following: (a) Mix 100 mL of rubbing alcohol with 40 mL of water. (b) Mix 100 mL of rubbing alcohol with 50 mL of water. (c) Add 140 mL of water to 70 grams of sugar and stir until the sugar dissolves. (d) Prepare a saturated solution of salt by adding 74 grams of kosher salt to 200 mL of water. Stir until no more salt will dissolve. It might be a good idea to leave this solution overnight to be sure as much salt as possible has dissolved. Some salt may remain undissolved.

4. Find the density of each liquid you prepared by measuring its mass and volume.

5. Prepare a data table similar to Table 1.

6. Test each sample by submerging a piece of the plastic in each liquid. Be sure to submerge it; surface tension might prevent it from sinking. In each of the liquids whose density you know, which plastics sink? Which float? In the blank spaces in the table under each type of plastic, write an F or an S depending on whether the plastic floats (F) or sinks (S) in the liquid.

What is the approximate density of each type of plastic? Which plastic is the most dense? Which is the least dense? **Save the plastic pieces for Experiment 1.5.**

Table 1:
A data table for Experiment 1.4

Liquid used	Density of liquid	PLASTICS					
		1 (PET)	2 (HDPE)	3 (PVC)	4 (LDPE)	5 (PP)	6 (PS)
alcohol							
alcohol + water (100:40)							
alcohol + water (100:50)							
cooking oil							
water	1.0 g/mL						
sugar water							
salt water							

Ideas for Science Fair Projects

- Do an experiment to determine the approximate density of Plexiglas®.
- In an effort to conserve energy, appear "green," and reduce additions to landfills, many fast-food businesses have switched from number 6 plastic containers for foods to paper. Does this switch really conserve energy, reduce landfill waste, and make America greener?

1.5 Do Plastics Burn?
(An Experiment)

Things YOU will Need:

☑ an adult
☑ small pieces of each type of plastic (numbers 1–7) used in Experiment 1.4
☑ kitchen sink
☑ matchless gas lighter such as one used to light outside gas cooking grills
☑ forceps

What happens to discarded plastics? Some, as you know, may be recycled. Others get buried in landfills. Some are sent to waste-to-energy plants, where trash is burned to generate electricity.

Do you think plastics will burn? Form a hypothesis. Then do this experiment.

Because a flame is used in this experiment, you should work with an adult.

1. Obtain a small piece of each of the seven kinds of plastic you used in Experiment 1.4.

2. Do this experiment in a kitchen sink. That way, should any plastic burn, you can extinguish it with a stream of water.

3. For a flame, use a matchless gas lighter such as one used to light gas cooking grills.

4. Use forceps to hold a small piece of number 1 plastic (PET) in the flame of a matchless gas lighter (see Figure 4). Does the plastic burn?

5. Repeat the experiment for small pieces of number 2, number 3, number 4, number 5, number 6, and number 7 plastics. Do all of these plastics burn? Can plastics sent to a waste-to-energy power plant be used to heat water to make steam?

Figure 4

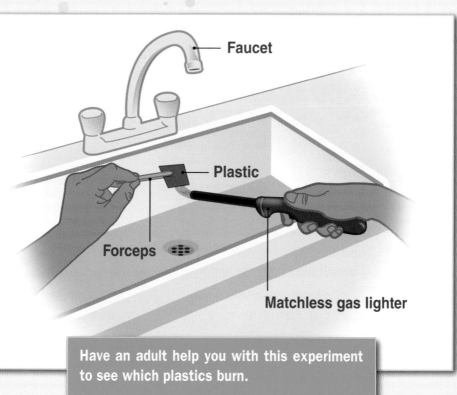

Faucet

Plastic

Forceps

Matchless gas lighter

Have an adult help you with this experiment to see which plastics burn.

Idea for a Science Fair Project

Design an experiment to determine the heat produced per gram of each of the seven types of plastic. Under adult supervision, carry out the experiments. Which plastic provides the most heat per gram?

The North Pacific Garbage Patch

In the north-central Pacific Ocean, there is a region known as the North Pacific Garbage Patch or the Pacific Trash Vortex. It has an area greater than that of Texas and California combined. More than 100 million tons of plastic and other debris have been carried there by ocean currents and wind. Four-fifths of the trash is believed to have come from the coastal areas of Japan and North America. The rest is from ships at sea. During an average week, an ocean liner carrying 3,000 passengers will toss eight tons of solid waste into the sea.

The North Pacific Garbage Patch consists primarily of tiny pieces suspended just below the water's surface. These submerged pieces are so small, they are invisible. They are often eaten by fish and other sea creatures and enter the food chain. The plastic contains toxic chemicals such as PCBs (polychlorinated biphenyls) and DDT (dichlorodiphenyltrichloroethane). When consumed by animals, including humans, they can cause a variety of illnesses, such as cancer.

Several organizations are studying ways to clean up this gigantic garbage patch. The task is challenging. And if it is successful, what can be done to prevent its reoccurrence?

Solid Waste

and

Decomposition

From about the time of the landing of the Pilgrims until well into the twentieth century, solid waste was burned or thrown into dumps in unpopulated areas considered unfit for building. Such areas included swamps, bogs, marshes, riverbanks, and wetlands. Over time, harmful residues from all this waste passed through the soil. It went into the groundwater, contaminating public and private drinking water.

At some dumps, flammable waste was burned. The polluted smoke engulfed nearby homes. Fires caused by escaping embers were so frequent that they were used to train apprentice firemen. Later, local pilots were using smoky dump fires to navigate.

In cities, garbage collected in the streets. By the late eighteenth century, New York City stank. Garbage and horse manure fouled the streets. (Remember, transportation within cities was by horse-drawn trolleys, carts, or carriages.) Conditions became so bad that the city formed the nation's first public garbage collecting system, and in 1885 America's first incinerator was built on Governors Island. The garbage was transferred to scows (flat-bottomed boats) in the Hudson River. The scows were towed out to sea, where the garbage was dumped. People known as scow trimmers combed the boats for clothes, metals, and other items they could collect and sell. Scow trimmers were America's first major recyclers.

As the country's population grew, so did the size of its dumps. In response, many cities built incinerators, where much of the solid waste was burned. In some regions, the burning trash was used to heat water, creating steam that was used to heat buildings or to turn turbines that generated electricity. In 1970, air pollution, partly from trash burning, led Congress to pass the Clean Air Act. The law forced many incinerators to shut down. Although this helped clear the air, landfills where waste materials were buried in soil grew larger. These landfills often polluted surrounding soil and groundwater.

The culture of late-twentieth-century America, known as the Throwaway Society, compounded the garbage problem. People were encouraged to buy the new and discard the old. The old things—bottles, paper, plastics, tires, carpets, appliances, food waste, clothes, trash of all kinds—were added to growing landfills. Over time, landfills became environmental hazards. Huge mounds of earth-covered, slowly decomposing waste were polluting the soil. Liquids from landfills were seeping into aquifers (underground water supplies) that provided drinking water. It became clear that humans were ruining the only planet we have. People began to realize that we needed to treat Earth in a greener, kinder way. Earth's resources and its tolerance for human activity are not unlimited.

Much of the material that goes to landfills to be buried can be recycled (used again). Recycling or reusing as many things as possible reduces the trash going to landfills. It also saves energy by reducing the demand for electrical and other forms of energy. For example, we can use recycled paper to make new paper. Recycled paper requires 30 percent less energy than making it from wood pulp. It also reduces air pollution by 70 percent.

If you reduce, reuse, and recycle as much as possible, you can help cut down on the amount of trash going to landfills.

2.1 **Landfill Pollution** (A Model)

Things YOU will Need:
- ✓ dry sand
- ✓ large, clear plastic vial (30–50 mL)
- ✓ eyedropper
- ✓ water
- ✓ green food coloring

Early landfills were simply land where people dumped garbage and trash. To reduce odors and to speed decomposition, sand, gravel, or other soil was used to cover the solid waste. To see what happened when pollutants were dumped in these early landfills, you can build a model landfill and add a "pollutant."

1. Add dry sand to a large, clear plastic vial until it is nearly full.

2. Use an eyedropper to "rain" on the sand. Watch the water trickle down through the sand to form groundwater at the bottom of the "landfill." Continue "raining" until a shallow "pond" covers the landfill.

3. Make a "well" at one side of the landfill (see Figure 5). To make the well, push an eyedropper to the bottom of the vial at one side of the "landfill." It can represent the well of a city's public water or of a homeowner who lives near the landfill.

4. Now, use the eyedropper to "pump" water from the well.

Figure 5

"pond"

"well"

"landfill"

A model of a landfill and a nearby well.

5. Assume there is a drought. No more water enters the landfill. Keep pumping water. What happens to the water level in the landfill?

6. Next, "pollute" the landfill. Add one or two drops of green food coloring to the sand.

7. "Rain" clear water onto the landfill again. What happens to the "pollution?"

8. Pump the well again.

9. Rain on and pump the landfill several times. Does the well become polluted?

10. Can the pollution be removed by many rains and pumpings?

How might a polluted aquifer be cleaned up?

Ideas for Science Fair Projects

- Make a model to show how water gets to your water faucets.

- Make a model to show what happens to your home's wastewater.

2.2 Build a Better Landfill (A Model)

Things YOU will Need:

- ✓ dry sand
- ✓ large, clear plastic vial (30–50 mL)
- ✓ clear, plastic container larger than vial
- ✓ eyedropper
- ✓ water
- ✓ green food coloring

When landfills are carefully planned, pollution from the landfill can be greatly reduced. To prevent pollutants from leaching (seeping) into nearby soil, landfills are lined with a thick plastic sheet. (In this case, plastic helps the environment—it's a green role for plastic.)

To see how this sheet prevents pollutants from leaching into nearby wells, you can make a model like the one shown in Figure 6.

1. Add dry sand to a clear plastic vial until it is about three quarters full. The vial of sand represents a landfill that lies within a plastic barrier.

2. Put the vial in a larger, clear plastic container.

3. Add sand to the larger container until it surrounds the "landfill." The sand in this larger container represents soil outside the landfill.

4. Use an eyedropper to "rain" on the sand in both the landfill and the surrounding soil. Watch the water trickle down through the sand to form groundwater at the bottom of the

Figure 6

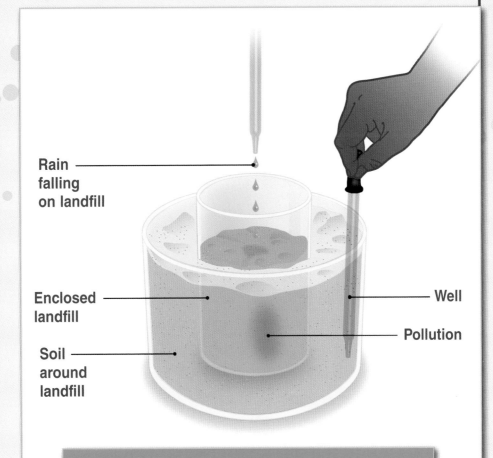

Rain falling on landfill

Enclosed landfill

Soil around landfill

Well

Pollution

A model of a plastic-lined landfill and a nearby well.

soil in and around the landfill. Continue "raining" until a thin "pond" covers the land surrounding the landfill.

5. Use an eyedropper to make a "well" at one side of the landfill in the soil outside the landfill. This well represents the well for a city's public water or for a homeowner living near the landfill. Pump water from the well until the "pond" disappears.

6. "Pollute" the landfill by adding one drop of green food coloring to it.

7. "Rain" clear water onto the landfill and surrounding soil again. What happens to the "pollution?" Does it reach the land surrounding the landfill?

8. Pump the well again.

9. Rain on the land surrounding the landfill and pump the well a few times. Does the well become polluted?

Charge More for More Trash?

Some communities believe that one way to reduce the trash sent to landfills is to charge households according to the volume of trash they generate. Instead of a single charge for all, those leaving two bags of trash for collection are charged twice as much as those who leave a single bag. This "pay as you throw" (PAYT) approach was promoted as a way to increase recycling. Those who regard bottles, cans, paper, and plastic as trash rather than recyclables would have an economic motive to change their ways. On the other hand, opponents of PAYT claim that the charge will lead to illegal dumping and create more unsightly litter.

2.3 **Decomposers in Soil** (An Experiment)

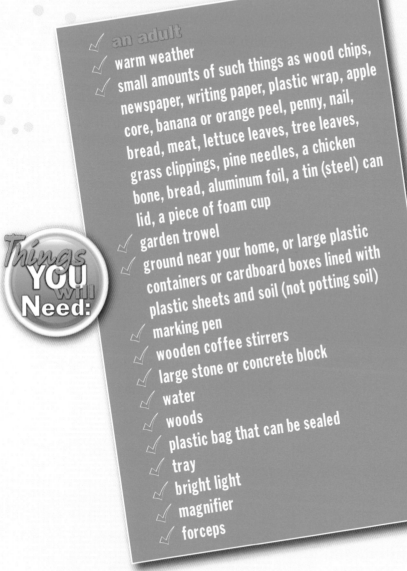

- an adult
- warm weather
- small amounts of such things as wood chips, newspaper, writing paper, plastic wrap, apple core, banana or orange peel, penny, nail, bread, meat, lettuce leaves, tree leaves, grass clippings, pine needles, a chicken bone, bread, aluminum foil, a tin (steel) can lid, a piece of foam cup
- garden trowel
- ground near your home, or large plastic containers or cardboard boxes lined with plastic sheets and soil (not potting soil)
- marking pen
- wooden coffee stirrers
- large stone or concrete block
- water
- woods
- plastic bag that can be sealed
- tray
- bright light
- magnifier
- forceps

Note: This experiment will take three months. Start when the weather is warm.

Some of the trash in landfills is biodegradable, some of it is not. Biodegradable substances can be broken down (decomposed) and returned to the earth. Micro-organisms that break down substances are called decomposers. Many of the fungi and bacteria found in soil can decompose many kinds of waste.

Which kinds of materials do you think will decompose in a landfill? Which will not? Form a hypothesis. Then do this experiment.

1. Gather small pieces of a number of things that are commonly thrown away. You might include some or all of the following: wood chips, newspaper, writing paper, plastic wrap, an apple core, a banana peel, bread, a penny, a nail, meat, lettuce, leaves, grass clippings, pine needles, a chicken bone, aluminum foil, a tin (steel) can lid, a foam cup, and other things. Be sure to include some things that you would classify as vegetable, plastic, paper, and metal.

2. In warm weather, use a garden trowel to dig a small hole in the ground near your home for each of the items you collected. Be sure to obtain permission before you dig any holes. Use labeled wooden coffee stirrers to identify where you buried each item. Food items can be placed in the same hole and covered with a large stone or concrete block so that animals cannot reach them. Make a map of your "burial ground."

   If you don't have an outside area where you can bury things, use some large plastic containers or line cardboard boxes with plastic. Add about 15 cm (6 inches) of garden soil (not potting soil) and bury the items in the soil. Use labeled coffee stirrers to mark where you buried each item. Add water to keep the soil damp but not wet.

3. After three or more months, carefully uncover the buried items. Which ones have decomposed or partially decomposed? Which items seem not to have decayed at all? Which substances do you think are biodegradable? Which do not appear to be biodegradable? What can be done with materials that do not decompose?

4. **With an adult's supervision**, go for a walk in the woods. Look for things that are undergoing decay. Can you find rotting leaves or pine needles? Look for them beneath newly fallen leaves and needles. Use a garden trowel to dig out some of the rotting leaves and a little of the soil beneath them. Place your diggings in a plastic bag and seal it.

5. Examine the contents on a tray in bright light. Use a magnifier and forceps to remove any animals you find. Can you find small roundworms? Earthworms? Insect larvae? Springtails? Ants? Spiders? Have you seen any of these animals in other places?

6. When you have finished examining the animals in the decaying leaves and soil, return the contents of your bag to the woods where you found them.

7. Look under and inside rotting logs and under rocks. How can you tell when wood is decaying? What kinds of animal and plant life do you find? Are any of the animals the same as those you found in decaying leaves? Would you expect to find these same animals on a lawn or in a meadow?

Idea for a Science Fair Project

Which will decompose faster if buried in soil, a cotton sock or nylon hose? Design and do an experiment to find out.

2.4 **Watching Things Decay** (An Observation)

You can actually watch things decompose.

1. Put pieces of bread, tomato, and crackers in a clear plastic box that has a lid. Add a few drops of water to each item and put the lid on the box.

2. Put the box in a moderately cool place (12–18°C, or 55–65°F) where you can watch it. After a few days, you will probably see bacterial colonies, mold, and various other fungi growing on the food. Molds reproduce by releasing tiny spores. Each spore can grow into a new mold and produce its own spores. Black spores will make the food look dark.

3. Continue to watch. Can you see the food gradually disappear as it is consumed by the decomposers? **Keep the lid on the box. Be careful not to breathe in mold spores or get them in your mouth!**

4. When you have seen food disappearing, place the covered box and its contents in a plastic bag. Seal the bag and place it in a trash can. This is one item you do not want to recycle!

5. **Wash your hands thoroughly in soap and water.**

2.5 **Water and Decay**
(An Experiment)

✓ dry foods such as cookies, dry cereal, and dog biscuits
✓ 2 plastic boxes with clear covers
✓ water
✓ a cool place
✓ plastic trash bag
✓ trash can

Things YOU will Need:

Note: This experiment will take several months.

Do decomposers need water? Form a hypothesis. Then do this experiment.

1. Place a few dry foods such as a dry cookie, some dry cereal, and a piece of a dog biscuit in each of two plastic boxes.

2. To one of the containers add enough water to dampen each food item. Add no water to the second box.

3. Put clear covers on both boxes and place them where the temperature is moderately cool (12–18°C or 55–65°F). Watch them over the course of several months. What do you conclude? Was your hypothesis correct?

4. Put the covered boxes and their contents in a plastic bag. Seal the bag and place it in a trash can. Don't try to recycle these boxes. They may contain mold spores that should not be inhaled.

5. Wash your hands thoroughly in soap and water.

Ideas for a Science Fair Project

- Under adult supervision, design and carry out an experiment to find out whether light is needed for substances to decay. Based on your findings, what can you conclude about the type of living organisms that cause decay?

- Under adult supervision, design and carry out an experiment to find out how temperature affects the rate at which food decays.

2.6 What Redi Discovered
(An Experiment)

Until the seventeenth century, people believed in spontaneous generation. They believed that decaying, nonliving, organic matter created the life that fed on it, such as maggots, molds, and other fungi.

Francesco Redi (1626–1697) decided to test the idea of spontaneous generation by doing an experiment. You can re-create and carry out his experiment.

This investigation is best done in the summer when flies are abundant. You will need six canning jars that can be sealed and will not break when heated.

1. **Ask an adult** to heat the jars in a pressure cooker to sterilize them.

2. Cut each of two hot dogs into three equal pieces.

3. **Ask an adult** to prepare some boiling water. Place the hot dogs in the boiling water.

4. After the hot dogs have cooked for a few minutes, place the grasping parts of a pair of kitchen tongs in the boiling water. The hot water will sterilize the tongs.

5. Using the tongs, put a piece of hot dog into each of the sterilized jars. Quickly seal two of them by covering them securely with their lids so that nothing can enter the sterile vessels.

6. Cover the mouths of two other jars with gauze so that air can enter but flies can't.

7. Leave the remaining two jars open so that flies can enter. Put the jars outdoors in a place where flies can reach them. Leave the jars there.

8. Observe each jar carefully on a daily basis for several weeks. In which jars do you find maggots?

    Can you find fly eggs in or on any of the jars?

    In which jars does the meat slowly decay?

Maggots and Spores

Redi showed that maggots do not appear spontaneously on food. The maggots appear only if flies can lay their eggs on the food. However, the spores of molds and other fungi can fall onto food even if it is covered by gauze that flies cannot penetrate.

In which jars is meat being consumed by maggots?

What can you conclude from your observations? Does spontaneous generation take place when food is protected from insects and mold spores?

9. After you have collected your evidence, carefully discard the contents of each jar into the trash. Then thoroughly clean the jars and your hands with soap and hot water.

Remember Your Rs

To make the environment greener, remember the five Rs—Reduce, Reuse, Recycle, Rethink, and Respect. Reduce waste and the growth of landfills by reusing, recycling, and rethinking. For example, paper can be reused; it has two sides. Both sides can hold print or writing. Old envelopes can be used to make lists or to write notes. Once paper has been reused, it can be recycled. Put it in a recycling bin for curb pickup of recyclables, or take the bin to a recycling center. And rethink how you might use things rather than discarding them. Cardboard boxes can be reused to package gifts or for mailing items; plastic containers that are not recyclable can be used to store paper clips, thumb tacks, nails, craft supplies, coins, or food in a refrigerator. Someone who is artistic might make sculptures from items you might call trash.

The Greening

of Waste

In many places, solid waste that would normally go to landfills is burned to generate electrical energy. The solid waste is transported to power plants in trucks or on railroad cars. On what is called the tipping floor, the waste is unloaded and sorted. Bulky materials that can be recycled are removed.

A conveyer belt carries the remaining waste to a shredder, where it is cut into small pieces before passing under an electromagnet. The magnet pulls out certain metals, which are then recycled. The remaining shredded waste, which is called refuse-derived fuel, contains a large amount of matter that will burn. The heat released by burning this fuel is used to boil water and generate steam. The steam turns the blades of a turbine that drives a generator, producing electrical energy. Ashes that collect at the bottom of the boiler are separated. Magnets remove some of the remaining metals and screening separates other metals. The metals are sold to scrap dealers for recycling. What is left is a gravel-like matter that is mixed with concrete and asphalt. The remaining ash is collected and sent to a landfill to be buried. Incinerator gases pass through scrubbers that remove some, but not all, of the pollutants in them before they are released into the atmosphere.

Waste-to-energy plants accomplish two major green objectives. (1) They reduce the waste sent to landfills. (2) They reduce America's dependence on fossil fuels (coal, oil, and natural gas) for generating electrical energy. However, burning trash, like burning fossil fuels, releases carbon dioxide, a greenhouse gas that contributes to global warming. It also releases other gases and particles that pollute the air.

This waste-to-energy plant in Germany burns trash to create electrical energy.

Some have suggested using solid waste to produce alcohol for gasohol (a fuel that is 90 percent gasoline and 10 percent alcohol). However, separating components that could not be used is probably too costly. And, strangely, there may not be enough trash. The estimated volume of accessible trash is about one-tenth that of the corn, switchgrass, and other organic matter presently used to make gasohol.

RECYCLE

3.1 Waste to Energy: An Electric Generator
(A Demonstration)

Things YOU will Need:

- ✓ an adult
- ✓ small toy electric motor (buy at an electronics store, hobby shop, toy store, or science supply company, or buy an old toy from a garage sale)
- ✓ 2 insulated wires with clips
- ✓ ammeter that measures milliamps or microamps
- ✓ bicycle
- ✓ gloves
- ✓ 1.2-volt flashlight bulb
- ✓ bulb holder
- ✓ thick rubber or plastic tubing with a very small inside diameter
- ✓ sharp knife

In a waste-to-energy power plant, steam is used to run a turbine that turns an electric generator. To see how this works, a toy electric motor can serve as a small generator. The electric motor has a coil of wire that turns between magnets. When the coils turn, the magnetic field through the wire coils changes. This causes electric charges to flow along the coils and out through connecting wires. The motor becomes a small electric generator.

1. Examine a small electric motor. There should be two small metal leads outside the metal case. These leads are connected to the motor's coil. Use two insulated wires with alligator clips to connect the motor's two leads to the poles of an ammeter that measures milliamps or microamps. Electric currents (moving charges) are measured in units called amperes. A milliamp is one thousandth of an ampere. A microamp is one millionth of an ampere.

2. You don't need a turbine to turn the coil in this generator. You can spin the motor's shaft with your fingers. When you do so, is an electric current generated? What happens if you turn the shaft faster? What happens if you spin it in the opposite direction? Can you explain what you see?

3. You can make a more continuous electric current. Turn a bicycle upside down. The bicycle's spinning wheel can serve as a turbine that turns the generator's coils. Give the front wheel a good spin. Hold the ammeter connected to the generator (electric motor) while **an adult**, wearing a glove, holds the generator's shaft against the spinning tire (see Figure 7). Does using the spinning wheel to turn the generator's shaft generate an electric current?

4. Connect the generator's leads to a 1.2-volt flashlight bulb in a bulb holder. Again, **ask an adult**, wearing a glove, to hold the motor's shaft against the side of a spinning bike tire. Can enough current be generated to light the bulb?

5. You may have to increase the friction between the spinning tire and the generator's shaft to make the generator's coils spin fast enough to light the bulb. To do this, slide thick rubber or plastic tubing with a small inside diameter over the shaft. Cut it to the same length as the shaft. The additional friction should enable you to light the 1.2-volt flashlight bulb.

Figure 7

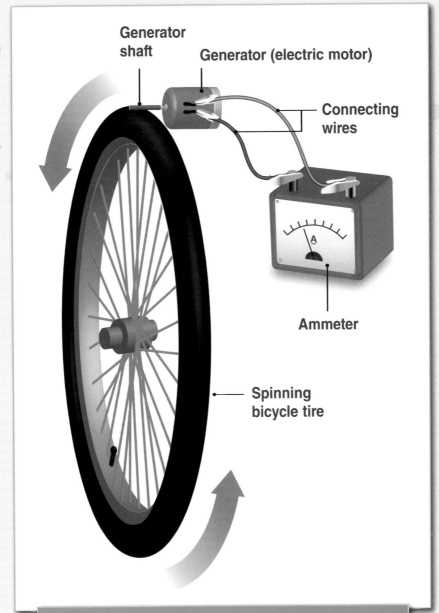

Generator shaft

Generator (electric motor)

Connecting wires

Ammeter

Spinning bicycle tire

A wire coil spinning between the poles of a magnet will produce an electric current.

Ideas for Science Fair Projects

- Figure out a way to generate a steady ongoing electric current from your small-motor generator.

- How will increasing the diameter of the generator's shaft affect its rate of rotation? Will it make the shaft spin faster or slower? Do an experiment to find out.

3.2 Composting
(An Activity)

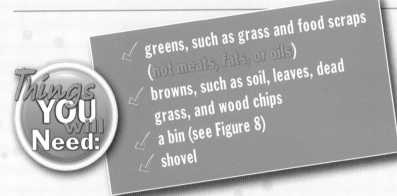

The fruits and vegetables that we eat, and the grass, trees, and other plants that grow, obtain their nutrients from the soil. These nutrients can be recycled. Don't send food scraps off to a landfill in a garbage truck. Those apple cores, orange peels, potato skins, coffee grounds, tea bags, and other food waste can be recycled by adding them to a compost bin.

Decomposers, such as bacteria and fungi, helped by insects and worms, can turn such food waste into nutrient-rich soil that can be used to grow new plants. A compost pile is an inexpensive way to make good, rich, garden soil from matter that you might otherwise throw away.

Composting will reduce the amount of waste you discard, conserve water, eliminate chemical fertilizers, and promote plant growth. Reducing waste can slow the growth of a landfill. Moist compost will reduce the need to water gardens. Avoiding chemical fertilizers will prevent contamination of groundwater. Growing more plants will help to remove carbon dioxide, a

Figure 8

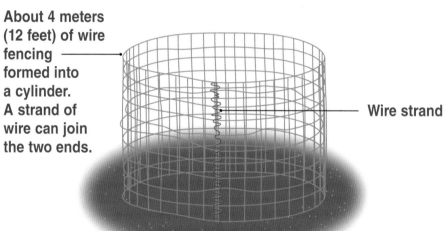

a)

Cover

Plastic trash can with holes drilled to admit air

Bottom can be buried a few inches in the soil.

b)

About 4 meters (12 feet) of wire fencing formed into a cylinder. A strand of wire can join the two ends.

Wire strand

8. a) An old plastic trash barrel with holes drilled in its side can serve as a bin. Cut off the bottom and bury the lower few inches of the barrel in soil.

b) Fencing wire with 2-inch by 4-inch (or smaller) openings can form a cylinder to hold the compost.

greenhouse gas, from the air. You can grow some of your food in a garden using compost as fertilizer.

Composting ingredients can be simplified into "greens" and "browns." Greens are fresh, damp materials such as green grass and food scraps (not meats, fats, or oils). Browns are dry matter such as soil, leaves, dead grass, and wood chips.

1. Start a compost pile by collecting as many greens and browns as possible. Place them in a pile or in a bin. (See Figure 8 for two ways to make a composting bin.) Some communities sell manufactured composting bins at reduced prices.

Composting is a great way to reduce the amount of trash you create. Compost can be used to help plants grow.

2. Keep the compost moist but not wet.

3. To speed the process: (a) Break the ingredients into small pieces. This increases their surface area, providing more contact between ingredients and the organisms that act on them. (b) Mix the pile occasionally by turning and stirring the ingredients with a shovel. This will increase exposure to air and the action of aerobic bacteria.

4. Once the compost becomes similar to soil, work it into your garden or flower bed. It contains the nutrients plants need to grow. Using compost instead of commercial fertilizers is a green way to garden.

3.3 Composting with Earthworms
(An Activity)

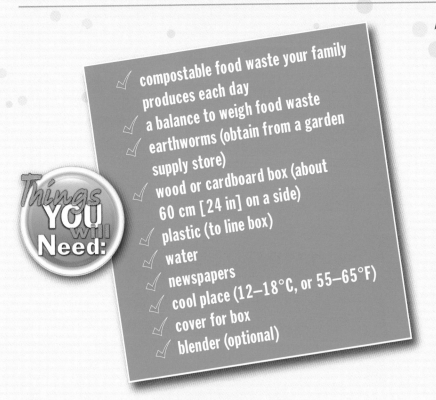

Things YOU will Need:

- ✓ compostable food waste your family produces each day
- ✓ a balance to weigh food waste
- ✓ earthworms (obtain from a garden supply store)
- ✓ wood or cardboard box (about 60 cm [24 in] on a side)
- ✓ plastic (to line box)
- ✓ water
- ✓ newspapers
- ✓ cool place (12–18°C, or 55–65°F)
- ✓ cover for box
- ✓ blender (optional)

Earthworms will eat and digest the organic matter found in food waste. An earthworm's digestive tract includes a gizzard where ingested food is ground by tiny stones. The worms excrete castings rich in nutrients that plants need to grow.

1. Collect and weigh the compostable food waste your family produces each day for a week (not meat, fats, or oils). Find the average weight produced per day.

2. Order earthworms from a garden supply store. The weight of the worms should be twice the average weight of food your family discards each day.

3. Find a wood or cardboard box that is about 60 cm (24 in) on a side. Line it with plastic.

4. Prepare a bed for the worms by filling the box with moist (not wet) shredded newspapers. Put the box in a place that is moderately cool (12–18°C, or 55–65°F).

5. Put the worms in the box. Cover the box. Feed the worms your family's daily food waste, but **DO NOT** include meat, dairy products, fats, or oils. If possible, grind the food waste in a blender before adding it to the box. This will increase the surface area of the scraps.

6. After two months, move the worms and bedding to one side of the box. Put fresh, moist, shredded newspaper on the other side.

7. Begin adding your daily garbage to the fresh bedding. After the worms move to the newly added paper, remove the castings from the other side of the box.

8. Spread the castings on potted plants or flower beds. The castings can also be used as soil for seedling plants.

3.4 Surface Area and Volume

(A Demonstration)

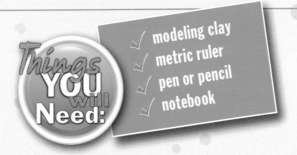
Breaking compost material into small pieces increases their surface area and speeds the composting process. To see how cutting ingredients into smaller pieces increases surface area, you can do this demonstration.

1. Use modeling clay to prepare a cube that is 2 cm on a side (see Figure 9a). What is the volume of this cube in cubic centimeters (cm^3)? What is the total surface area of this cube in square centimeters (cm^2)?

2. Use modeling clay to prepare cubes that are 1 cm on a side (see Figure 9b). What is the volume of one such cube? Make enough cubes 1 cm on a side so that their total volume equals that of the cube 2 cm on a side. How many 1 cm^3 cubes did you make?

3. What is the total surface area of all the cubes that are 1 cm on a side?

4. What is the ratio of surface area to volume for the cube 2 cm on a side? What is the ratio of surface area to volume for the cube 1 cm on a side?

What happens to the surface area when big pieces of matter are cut into smaller pieces? (See page 73 at the end of the chapter for answers.)

Figure 9

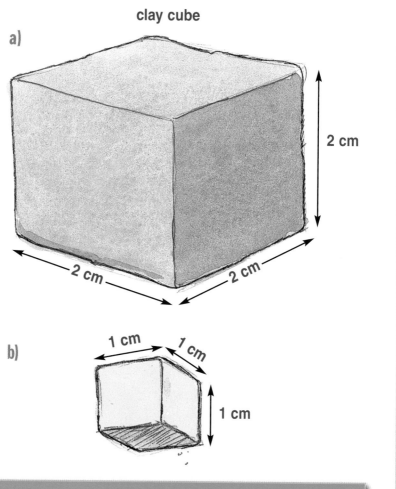

clay cube

a)

2 cm

2 cm

2 cm

b)

1 cm

1 cm

1 cm

9. a) A clay cube two centimeters on a side.
   b) A clay cube one centimeter on a side. How many of these equal the volume of the cube two centimeters on a side?

3.5 Polluting Substances Measured in Parts Per Million

(An Activity)

Things YOU will Need:

- ✓ plastic ice cube tray
- ✓ green or blue food coloring
- ✓ eyedropper
- ✓ cold tap water
- ✓ toothpicks

As you have seen, a landfill can pollute an aquifer that provides drinking water. A local water department listed hazardous substances in a chart similar to the one on the next page. The unit *ppm* means "parts per million," *ppb* means "parts per billion." One ppm is the equivalent of 1 penny in $10,000; one ppb corresponds to 1 penny in $10,000,000. Chemists are able to measure such small concentrations.

Because of a leaking tank at a nearby gasoline station, a citizen with a private well had his water tested for VOCs (volatile organic compounds). The test indicated a benzene concentration of 50 ppm. His neighbor's well tested at 5,500 ppm. Should either or both homeowners stop drinking his well water?

Is the water provided by this water department safe to drink?

Contaminant	Unit used to measure	Maximum concentration found in water samples	Maximum allowed for safe drinking
lead	ppb	7	15
copper	ppm	0.61	1.3
tetrachloroethylene	ppb	1.8	5
nitrate	ppm	0.19	10
chlorine	ppm	0.34	4
benzene	ppb	0.0	5

One way to get a sense of what one part per million looks like is to add one drop of food coloring to 999,999 drops of water. That would be a tedious process. Assume that there are 20 drops in a milliliter (mL). If we had one drop (0.05 mL) of food coloring, we would have to add 50,000 mL (50 L, or 13.2 gal) of water because:

999,999 drops/ 20 drops/ mL = 50,000 mL =
50 liters = 13.2 gallons

Fortunately, there is an easier way to see what a dilution of 1:1,000,000 looks like.

1. Find a clean, dry plastic ice cube tray. You would normally fill the tray's cavities with water and place the tray in a freezer. This time, add a few drops of green or blue food coloring to one of the cavities.

2. Use an eyedropper to add one drop of the food coloring to a second cavity.

3. Thoroughly rinse the eyedropper with running water. Then use the eyedropper to add 9 drops of water to the one drop of food coloring (see Figure 10). Stir with a toothpick. The concentration of the food coloring is now 1/10 of its initial concentration, a dilution of 1:10.

4. Thoroughly rinse the eyedropper in running water. Then use the eyedropper to add one drop of the 1:10 diluted food coloring to a third cavity. Thoroughly rinse the eyedropper with running water. Then use the eyedropper to add 9 drops of water to the one drop of diluted food coloring from step 3. Stir with a fresh toothpick. The concentration of the food coloring is now 1/100 of its initial concentration, a 1:100 dilution.

5. Thoroughly rinse the eyedropper in running water. Then use the eyedropper to add one drop of the 1:100 diluted food coloring to a fourth cavity. Thoroughly rinse the eyedropper with running water. Then use the eyedropper to add 9 drops of water to the one drop of diluted food coloring from step 4. Stir with a fresh toothpick. The concentration of the food coloring is now 1/1,000 of its initial concentration, a 1:1,000 dilution.

6. Thoroughly rinse the eyedropper in running water. Then use the eyedropper to add one drop of the 1:1,000 diluted food coloring to a fifth cavity. Thoroughly rinse the eyedropper with running water. Then use the eyedropper to add 9 drops of water to the one drop of diluted food coloring from step 5. Stir with a fresh toothpick. The concentration of the food coloring is now 1/10,000 of its initial concentration, a 1:10,000 dilution.

Figure 10

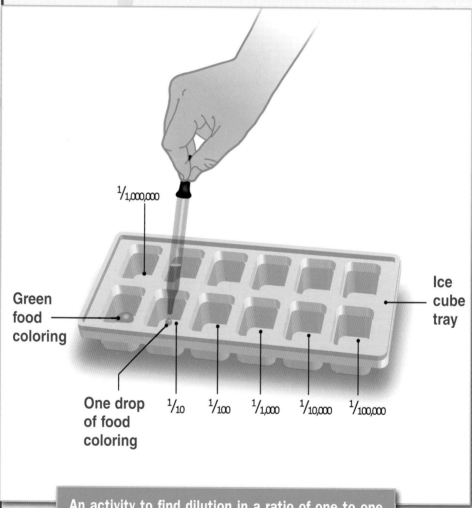

$^1/_{1,000,000}$

Green food coloring

Ice cube tray

One drop of food coloring

$^1/_{10}$ $^1/_{100}$ $^1/_{1,000}$ $^1/_{10,000}$ $^1/_{100,000}$

An activity to find dilution in a ratio of one to one million (1:1,000,000)

7. Thoroughly rinse the eyedropper in running water. Then use the eyedropper to add one drop of the 1:10,000 diluted food coloring to a sixth cavity. Thoroughly rinse the eyedropper with running water. Then use the eyedropper to add 9 drops of water to the one drop of diluted food coloring from step 6. Stir with a fresh toothpick. The concentration of the food coloring is now 1/100,000 of its initial concentration, a 1:100,000 dilution.

8. Finally, rinse the eyedropper in running water once more. Then use the eyedropper to add one drop of the 1:100,000 diluted food coloring to a seventh cavity. Thoroughly rinse the eyedropper with running water. Then use the eyedropper to add 9 drops of water to the one drop of diluted food coloring from step 7. Stir with a fresh toothpick. The concentration of the food coloring is now 1/1,000,000 of its initial concentration.

It has the same appearance as it would have if you added 999,999 drops to one drop of the food coloring. Can you still detect color in the 1:1,000,000 dilution?

Green Tips

People tend to think that waste is inexpensive and that landfills are an efficient way to take care of it. They would change their minds if they were charged for the actual cost of global warming, groundwater and air pollution, and for the depletion of such resources as forests, bauxite, iron ore, and fossil fuels. The following tips offer easy ways to reduce these hidden costs of waste.

● Recycle paper and buy recycled-paper products. It saves trees that would be cut and made into paper. And trees, as you may know, remove carbon dioxide, a greenhouse gas, from the air. As a result, using recycled paper products can help to reduce global warming.

- Use recycled-paper tissues, which are oxygen-bleached. Some are as soft as tissues regularly sold, which are bleached with chlorine.

- Use cloth napkins and towels rather than paper.

- Use permanent dishes and cutlery instead of plastic or paper.

- Nearly 300 million plastic bags are used in the United States each day. Only about 2 percent are recycled. Use your own canvas bags rather than the store's plastic bags when grocery shopping. Many stores encourage this and give a small discount for doing so.

- Ask if your school uses recycled paper for stationery, photocopiers, and printers. If not, encourage the school to do so. It will save energy and trees and reduce pollution. Also encourage your school to purchase recycled supplies such as pens, pencils, scissors, rulers, etc.

- Use pens that can be refilled with ink. More than a billion ballpoint pens find their way to landfills each year.

- Use an aluminum or stainless steel water bottle to carry liquids to school and on long walks, bike rides, and trips. Avoid bottled water, which comes in plastic bottles that often aren't recycled. And, in fact, bottled water is no healthier than most public water.

- Tons of batteries are discarded every year in landfills. Use rechargeable batteries and wind-up (crank) radios. Take used batteries to a recycling facility.

- To reduce solid waste at landfills, use biodegradable bags and cloths.

- You can smell mothballs because they release naphthalene or dichlorobenzene, which are toxic vapors. You can repel moths with natural products such as cedar disks, lavender bags, or a mix of herbs and spices such as cinnamon, cardamom, and rosemary.

- Use homemade cleaners that are nontoxic and biodegradable.

- Buy products that are in recyclable glass or plastic bottles.

- Hang a cloth towel by the sink. Use the cloth towel, not a paper towel, after hand washing.

- Save plastic bags. They can be used again. Turn dirty ones inside out, wash them and hang them up to dry.

- Reuse aluminum foil. Wash it; dry it; reuse it. When it can't be reused, recycle it.

Greenwashing

Some products that claim to be green or eco-friendly may cover up contents or actions that are actually harmful to the environment. Such actions are called "greenwashing."

In November 2007, TerraChoice Environmental Marketing Inc. listed "The Six Sins of Greenwashing™."

(1) The Hidden Trade-off occurs when products base their "green" claim on only one factor; for example, when products called "energy-efficient" are made with hazardous materials.

(2) No proof of claim is when there is no certification for a particular claim that a product is, for example, organic or chemical-free.

(3) Vagueness claims are claims so general as to be misleading. For example, "natural" products may not be healthy. Arsenic is natural but also harmful.

(4) Irrelevance exists when a claim no longer has meaning. For example, a product might claim to be free of chlorofluorocarbons (CFCs), which were banned in the 1970s.

(5) Lesser of two evils involves promotion for harmful products such as organic cigarettes or a green pesticide.

(6) Fibbing occurs when a product is falsely claimed to be certified by a well-known standard such as Energy Star.

Answers to Demonstration 3.4 Surface Area and Volume

1. The volume of the cube 2 cm on a side is 2 cm $\times$ 2 cm $\times$ 2 cm = 8 cm^3. Its surface area is 2 cm $\times$ 2 cm = 4 cm^2 per side. There are six sides, so the total surface area is 24 cm^2.

2. The volume of each cube 1 cm on a side is 1 cm $\times$ 1 cm $\times$ 1 cm = 1 cm^3. You need to make 8 such cubes to equal the volume of the cube 2 cm on a side.

3. The total surface area of these 8 cubes 1 cm on a side is 48 cm^2. Each cube has 6 faces, and each face has an area of 1 cm^2 (1 cm $\times$ 1 cm). The area of the 6 faces on each cube is 6 cm^2. The surface area of all 8 cubes is 8 $\times$ 6 cm^2 = 48 cm^2.

4. The ratio of surface area to volume for the large cube is 24/8 = 3/1 = 3. For the small cube the surface area to volume ratio is 6/1 = 6. Breaking matter into smaller pieces increases the ratio of surface area to volume.

More Things to Recycle

Many things can be recycled. The most common household recyclables are paper, glass, plastic, aluminum cans, steel cans, and yard waste. Steel cans are often called tin cans because they are coated with a thin layer of tin. The tin prevents the steel from rusting.

Beyond household recycling, scrap metal is a major recycling industry. Old cars, trucks, bridges, and other sources of steel are recycled to provide the metal found in machines and other steel products. Copper pipes and wire are also recycled.

Metals

The two most commonly recycled household metals are aluminum and iron (steel cans). Both are abundant as metallic ores (natural materials in Earth's crust from which metals can be obtained). A lot of energy is required to extract these two metals from their ores.

Iron (Steel)

Steel, which is mostly iron, is widely used in making all kinds of machinery. In American kitchens, it is the main metal in food cans and appliances. Steel is made in a blast furnace. Iron ore, limestone, and coke (a form of carbon) are added at the top of the huge furnace. Preheated oxygen is blown in at the bottom. As the iron melts, it drips down into a pit at the bottom of the furnace and is drawn off. Iron from the blast furnace is called pig iron. In addition to iron, it contains about 4 percent carbon, 2 percent silicon, 1 percent phosphorus, and traces of sulfur.

Steel is made in a blast furnace.

Pig iron is refined into steel by burning out the impurities, leaving small amounts of carbon, which strengthens the steel.

Steel is also made by recycling scrap steel. Old and wrecked cars and car parts are sold to steel-shredding companies. The shredded steel, together with other scrap steel from buildings, ships, railroad tracks, and other sources, are shipped to steel companies and remelted to make new steel.

Recycling steel makes economic sense. It requires 74 percent less energy to make steel from recycled steel than from iron ore. It also requires 40 percent less water and generates 75 percent less air pollution.

Aluminum

Aluminum, a chemical element, is commonly used to make cans and foil in kitchens. But aluminum does not exist as an element (a substance with just one kind of atom). It is made from bauxite (Al_2O_3), an ore made of aluminum (Al) and oxygen (O). Bauxite is mined primarily in Australia, Jamaica, Brazil, and western Africa. It is dug from the earth in open pits called strip mines. Making aluminum requires a great deal of energy. Even before the digging occurs, soil, trees, and rocks have to be cleared in order to reach the ore.

Once extracted, the bauxite is transported to a processing plant, where it is crushed into tiny pieces. The pieces are heated to remove water that is chemically attached to bauxite. The bauxite is further crushed into a fine white powder called alumina, which is melted in a smelter. After a rather complicated

Bottles, Cans, and Jars

During the late eighteenth and early nineteenth centuries, France and England were almost constantly at war with one another. Soldiers of both armies were plagued by food poisoning and malnutrition. The French offered a prize to anyone who could find a way to provide soldiers with food consistently safe to eat. In 1810, Nicolas Appert won the prize. He packed food in glass bottles that he cooked and then sealed with corks.

The English solved the problem in a different way. Peter Durand made cans from iron coated with tin. Food, sterilized by heating, was poured into the cans, which were then covered with tin-plated iron tops and soldered shut. English soldiers probably ate better than the French because, unlike Appert's glass containers, Durand's steel cans did not break.

chemical process, a strong electric current is used to separate the aluminum.

Pure aluminum is soft and weak. Small quantities of other elements are added to the molten metal to make it a strong, low-density metal alloy. The liquid aluminum alloy is poured into molds, where it cools and solidifies into ingots (bars) of various shapes. Later, the ingots are melted. Some melted ingots may be rolled into sheets of various thicknesses to make aluminum foil, cans, or airplane bodies. Others may be made into wire or poured into molds to make kettles, pans, automobile parts, and other items. Aluminum is so versatile because it is strong but light, has a high melting point (658°C, or 1216°F), and is a good conductor of both heat and electricity.

Lead, Mercury, and Batteries

Electrodes in automobile and truck batteries and in the batteries of other vehicles such as golf carts are made of lead. Lead and its compounds are toxic; consequently, lead storage batteries should be recycled. During recycling, the lead electrodes are removed and melted before being made into new electrodes.

Smaller batteries that contain mercury or other heavy metals should be taken to a hazardous waste center, where they can be processed. Thermometers containing mercury should be handled in the same way. These hazardous thermometers can be replaced with alcohol or digital thermometers.

Metal Cans

At a processing center, metal cans are manually separated from other recyclables (paper, glass, and plastics). The aluminum and steel cans are then separated from one another by a process similar to the one you will carry out in Experiment 4.1.

Recycling of tin cans in America began during World War II. The Japanese controlled many of the countries where tin ores were mined. As a result, the United States turned to recycling as a major source of tin and steel.

In some states, a deposit of five or ten cents is made when a product is purchased in a steel or aluminum can. The deposit is refunded when the cans are returned. Once they are returned, the cans can be recycled.

4.1 Separating Aluminum and Steel "Cans"
(An Experiment)

Things YOU will Need:

- ✓ an adult
- ✓ gloves
- ✓ safety glasses
- ✓ top of a clean steel can
- ✓ ruler
- ✓ pair of metal-cutting shears or a heavy pair of ordinary shears
- ✓ kitchen counter or tray
- ✓ aluminum foil
- ✓ bar magnet, refrigerator magnet, or a stack of 4 or 5 square or round ceramic or rubberized magnets

When it comes to recycling cans, most curbside pickups or recycling centers do not require that steel and aluminum cans be separated. Billions of cans of both kinds are recycled each year. However, aluminum and steel cans are manufactured in very different ways so the two metals have to be separated before they can be used to make new cans or other articles of aluminum or steel.

How can aluminum and steel cans be separated? Form a hypothesis. Then do this experiment.

Ask an adult to help you. Both of you should **wear work gloves and safety glasses** because you will be handling sharp pieces of metal.

1. Find a steel can, such as a soup can. Steel cans are heavier than aluminum cans.

2. **Ask an adult** to help you cut the top or bottom of a steel can into small pieces, roughly 0.5 cm on a side. A pair of metal-cutting shears work best, but a heavy pair of ordinary shears will work **in adult hands**. Place the steel pieces on a tray.

3. Cut a dozen or more pieces, roughly a centimeter on each side, from a sheet of aluminum foil. Roll each piece into a small ball. Each ball can represent an aluminum can. Mix them with the pieces of steel that represent steel cans.

4. Hold a magnet in a gloved hand. Being careful not to touch them, move the magnet over the "cans" as shown in Figure 11.

   What happens? How do you think aluminum and steel cans are separated at a recycling center?

   Save the "cans." You will use them in the next experiment.

Ideas for Science Fair Projects

- Find a way to measure the density of aluminum and steel. Which metal is more dense? How many times more dense?

- Invent a method by which aluminum and steel cans might be separated because of their different densities.

Figure 11

Separating aluminum and steel "cans"

4.2 Separating Aluminum and Steel "Cans"
(A Demonstration)

Things YOU will Need:

- ✓ aluminum and steel "cans" from Experiment 4.1
- ✓ large steel nail
- ✓ enameled copper wire
- ✓ ruler
- ✓ 2 insulated wires
- ✓ D cell
- ✓ battery holder or a strong, wide rubber band

The recycling industry uses huge electromagnets to separate aluminum and steel cans. You can make a small electromagnet and use it to separate the "cans" you made in Experiment 4.1.

1. Try to separate the "cans" you made in Experiment 4.1 by moving a large steel nail over them.

2. Commercial electromagnets contain a soft-iron core, but you can use an ordinary large steel nail as a core. Wrap 100 turns of enameled copper wire around the nail. Always wrap in the same direction. Leave about 30 cm (1 ft) of wire at each end of the coil.

3. Use sandpaper to remove about 3 cm (1 in) of the enamel from each end of the wire.

4. Using insulated wires, connect the ends of the coil to opposite poles of a D cell. If you have a battery holder, you can easily connect the wires to the opposite poles of the D cell. If not, you can use a strong, wide, rubber band to hold the wires against the poles. Do not leave the wires connected for very long or you will wear out the D cell.

5. Move the end of the electromagnet over the "cans" as shown in Figure 12. What happens? What happens when you disconnect the electromagnet from the D cell?

6. Save the steel and aluminum pieces for Experiment 4.5.

Figure 12

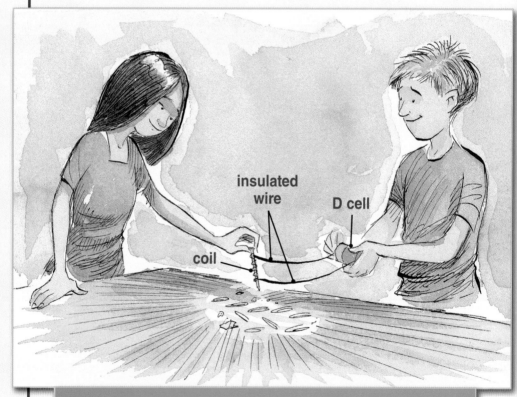

Use an electromagnet to separate aluminum from steel "cans."

Ideas for Science Fair Projects

- How many paper clips can your electromagnet lift? Remove 50 of the 100 turns of wire you used to make the coil. How many paper clips can your electromagnet lift now? How does the number of turns in the coil affect the strength of your electromagnet?

- Do an experiment to find out if the size of the core affects the strength of an electromagnet.

- How does the number of D cells affect the strength of your electromagnet?

- Try cores other than a steel nail, such as pencil leads, aluminum, copper, lead, glass, plastic, and so on. Do any of them improve the electromagnet's strength?

- Wind 50 turns of wire around the nail in one direction and 50 turns in the opposite direction. How does this affect the strength of your electromagnet? Can you explain why?

Glass

Think of all the ways in which we use glass. We drink from glass vessels, eat off glass plates, examine our facial images in glass mirrors, and look through glass spectacles, magnifying glasses, microscope and telescope lenses, as well as windows. We buy glass lightbulbs and foods and drinks in glass jars or bottles. We use glass fibers (fiber optics) in communication and in medical tools so that doctors can peer inside our bodies to observe or operate on internal organs. You may have traveled over crushed recycled glass that was mixed with petroleum to pave roads. In what other ways do we use glass? How many ways can you think of?

Glass was probably discovered by accident thousands of years ago. Someone built a very hot fire on sand and noticed the smooth, shiny globs that remained when the fire went out. We know that Egyptians were making glass vases, jewelry, and other objects as early as 1500 B.C. Ancient Romans made glass for windows, mirrors, prisms and magnifiers. By the sixteenth century, Dutch glass workers were making lenses for use in telescopes. When Galileo learned what the Dutch were doing, he built a telescope and turned it to the heavens. There he discovered craters on our Moon and more distant moons orbiting the planet Jupiter.

Glass is the perfect material to recycle because, unlike paper, it can be recycled forever.

E-Waste

Great Britain requires that discarded electronic devices such as cell phones and computers be recycled. Such e-waste contains copper, gold, silver, and platinum worth millions of dollars.

In Australia, an orchard uses discarded shells of Macintosh computers as nesting sites for birds that feed on insect pests.

While the wood fibers in paper weaken with re-peated recycling, glass can be crushed, remelted, and reshaped as many times as we wish.

Recycled glass is first sorted by color and then crushed into tiny pieces called cullet. It is cleaned, then sold to a glass factory, where it is mixed with sand and other silicates. It is turned into a liquid by heating, and shaped into new bottles, jars, and other glass products before it cools. Glass factories ship the new glass products to companies that use them for a variety of purposes. Commonly, glass jars are made to hold various foods and liquids.

In many states, you pay a refundable deposit of five or ten cents when you buy a product sold in a recyclable glass bottle or jar. While many bottles and jars are recyclable, lightbulbs, ceramics, dishes, drinking glasses, plate glass, windowpanes, and glass cookware are not.

Green Tips

- Whenever possible, purchase products in glass rather than plastic. Plastics are made from petroleum. More than half the petroleum used in the United States is purchased from foreign countries.

- Your family can buy many glass items at bargain prices from thrift shops. This saves money and serves to reuse the glass. Reciprocate by donating unwanted glass items to those shops so that the glass can be reused by others.

- Organize friends to help others, such as senior citizens, recycle glass. Your group could return bottles for their deposits, collect discarded bottles for recycling, and sponsor contests about ways to reuse glass products and reduce waste.

Glass can be recycled forever. It can be crushed and reshaped as many times as we want.

- Reuse glass products. Large jars can be used as vases, terrariums and door stops. Smaller jars can serve to hold pencils, pins, paper clips, or coins. They might also be used as candleholders and vases for small flowers. Glass fishbowls make very good enclosures for terrariums. Even pieces of broken colored glass, handled with heavy gloves, could be used to make mosaics and collages.

What other ways can you think of to reuse glass objects?

Paper

Paper is made of small wood or cotton fibers pressed tightly together. Wood fibers are found in less expensive paper, such as newspaper. Fibers from cotton rags are used to make fine-grade writing paper. Less expensive writing paper has a mixture of wood and cotton fibers.

Sizing is added when making writing paper and art paper. Sizing is a gel made of glue, wax, or clay. It is used to coat paper. The sizing fills the spaces between the fibers and makes the paper smooth. It also prevents ink from feathering—spreading as it moves between unsized fibers.

The wood fibers come from trees that are cut and transported to a mill. At the mill, machines strip away the bark from the log. The logs are then shredded into small pieces before pulping. Pulping takes place in a digester, where the wood chips are treated with chemicals. The chemicals remove the lignin that holds wood fibers together and makes them rigid. At this stage, other fibers such as cotton rags may be added to what has become a slurry of loose fibers in water. On its way to a mixer, the pulp is bleached. In the mixer, the

Paper in a papermill is dried and wound onto rollers. This paper will be used for newspaper.

pulp is beaten until it becomes very smooth. Fillers, such as china clay, colored pigments, and sizing, are added to improve smoothness and quality of the product. The smooth pulp is then fed to a flow box, where it is transferred to a moving mesh belt. Water drains through the mesh, and a roller presses the pulp's fibers into a sheet known as a web. Belts move the web between rollers that press and steam more water from the fibers. The web continues to move through a drier before the paper is wound onto rolls or cut into sheets.

4.3 Viewing Paper Fibers
(An Observation)

Things YOU will Need:
- ✓ paper towel
- ✓ strong magnifying glass or a low-power microscope
- ✓ water
- ✓ saucer
- ✓ food coloring

1. Make a small tear along the edge of a paper towel. Examine the tear with a strong magnifying glass or a low-power microscope. You will see the tiny, closely packed wood fibers.

2. Pour some water into a saucer. Add drops of food coloring. Touch the torn edge of the paper towel to the colored water. Using the magnifying glass, watch the water go into the paper. Water moves into the small spaces between the fibers by what is called capillary action.

4.4 Recycling Paper
(A Demonstration)

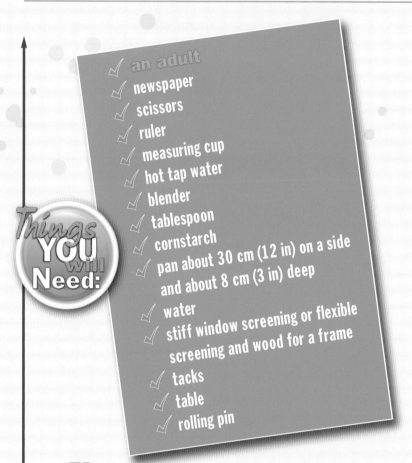
You can recycle some paper. Without the bleaching, sizing, pressing, and other processes that go on in a paper mill, you can't expect quality writing paper. However, this experiment will provide a basic understanding of how paper is recycled.

1. Cut a sheet of newspaper into square pieces roughly 1 cm (1/2 in) on a side. You do not need to be precise.

2. **Ask an adult** to help you turn the paper into pulp. Pour one cup of hot tap water into a blender. Then pour the paper you cut up into the blender.

3. Add 3 tablespoons of cornstarch to a second cup of hot water. Stir the mixture. Then add it to the blender.

4. **Ask the adult** to plug in the blender and turn it on. Let the blender chop and mix the paper and water until it looks like a thin gray gravy.

5. Find a pan that is about 30 cm (12 in) on a side and about 8 cm (3 in) deep. Add water to the pan. The water should be about 3–4 cm (1 1/2 in) deep.

6. Place a piece of stiff window screening in the pan. If you only have flexible screening, build a small wood frame that will fit inside the pan. Then stretch the screening across the frame and use tacks to hold it in place.

7. Put the screen in the pan. Be sure it is covered with water.

8. Pour one cup of the paper gravy from the blender over the screen. Spread it evenly across the screen with your fingers.

9. Lift the screen. Let the excess water drain into the pan.

10. Put a thick open newspaper on a table. Place the screen with the pulp on one page of the open newspaper.

11. Close the newspaper and carefully turn it over. The screen is now above the pulp.

12. Use a rolling pin or flat hands to squeeze water from the pulp. The newspaper above and below the pulp will absorb the water.

13. Open the newspaper. Leave the pulp untouched until it is dry. This may take a day or two.

14. When the pulp is dry, lift it from the screen. If the paper is very thick, you have made cardboard. Can you write on the paper or cardboard you made? How is this paper different from paper you normally write on? Why do you think it is different?

Ideas for Science Fair Projects

- Try making the paper without adding cornstarch. How does it compare with the paper you made with cornstarch?

- Investigate capillary action. How is the height to which water rises in narrow glass tubes related to the diameter of the tubes? Do an experiment to find out.

4.5 Separating Trash for Recycling
(An Experiment)

Things YOU will Need:

- ☑ aluminum and steel pieces from Experiment 4.1
- ☑ scissors
- ☑ small pieces of paper
- ☑ several paper clips
- ☑ rubber band
- ☑ several small marbles
- ☑ toothpick
- ☑ a plastic straw
- ☑ plate
- ☑ strong magnet or electromagnet
- ☑ rubber balloon
- ☑ dishpan
- ☑ water

How do you think mixed trash can be separated so that recyclables can be sent to processing centers? Form a hypothesis. Then do the following experiment.

This experiment should be done on a day in winter when humidity is very low.

If recyclables are to be salvaged before trash is buried or burned, the recyclables must be separated from the rest of the trash. Workers could separate recyclables piece by piece, but that would be slow and costly. Let's see how trash might be separated by machines.

1. Prepare a model of trash that might need to be separated. Include the aluminum and steel pieces from Experiment 4.1, small pieces of paper, several paper clips to represent other metal, a rubber band cut into pieces to represent rubber items such as tires, several small marbles to represent glass, pieces of a toothpick to represent wood, and small pieces of a plastic straw.

2. Mix this "trash" together on a plate.

3. Move a strong magnet or electromagnet over the trash. What materials are removed from the trash by the magnet?

4. Blow up a rubber balloon. Give the balloon an electric charge by rubbing it briskly on your hair or woolen clothing. The balloon represents a static-electric machine that could be moved over a mixture of real trash.

5. Move the balloon over the trash. What items are removed by the electric charge?

6. Dump the trash that remains into a dishpan. Add water. Which of the remaining trash items float? Which sink? How can the floaters and sinkers be separated? How can a mixture of floaters be separated? A mixture of sinkers?

4.6 Natural Resources Trapped in Solid Waste

(An Activity)

Things **YOU** will **Need:** ☑ solid waste from your home or school

The solid wastes that we discard were made from natural resources such as wood, metal ores, and petroleum.

1. Examine the kinds of solid waste from your home or school. They might include cans, newspapers, glass and plastic bottles, food, and other items.

2. Try to identify the natural resource from which each item was made.

Resources may be renewable or nonrenewable. Renewable resources can't be used up because they can be continually replaced. For example, energy generated by sunlight, wind, and moving water are renewable sources of energy. The wood used to make paper is a renewable resource provided care is taken to replace the trees as fast as or faster than they are used.

Nonrenewable resources are resources that cannot be replaced or whose replacement would take so long as to be impractical. They can be used up. For example, fossil fuels are considered nonrenewable because the formation of coal, oil, and natural gas from dead plants and animals takes millions of years. Bauxite and other metallic ores also take millions of years to form.

3. Reexamine the solid wastes from your home or school. Try to identify which are from renewable resources and which are from nonrenewable resources.

What Can YOU Do?

Recycling is one way to make a greener America. Making paper, glass, metal, and plastic products from recycled materials requires much less energy than making them from trees, sand, metal ores, and petroleum.

Neighborhoods and nations are more appealing when they are tidy and well kept. That is why some of the activities in this chapter are concerned with removing the unrecycled litter that detracts from the natural charm of a town, city, beach, or neighborhood.

Litter is not only unattractive, it can be harmful to both humans and animals. Toxic chemicals can poison animals and seep into the soil, polluting the water we drink. Small animals can get their head stuck in small containers when they try to eat food left inside. Animals may cut their tongue on opened cans; they may become sick or even die from eating cigarette butts, foam cups, or plastic wrap.

5.1 Organize a Litter Removal Squad

(An Activity)

You can improve the appearance of your neighborhood or school by organizing a litter squad or squads. At the same time, you may raise a little money.

1. Provide two large garbage bags for each squad. One member of the squad will carry the bags. In one bag, put items that are recyclable, such as cans, glass, and plastic containers. In the other bag, put trash that cannot be recycled.

2. Two or three other members of the squad, wearing work gloves, will pick up litter and put it into the bags.

3. An adult, such as a parent or teacher, should be available to pick up dangerous things such as broken glass and disposable syringes. Dangerous material should be placed in paper bags and then deposited in a separate garbage bag.

Figure 13

Plastic

Cans

Paper

Glass

Separate litter for recycling or for a landfill or transfer station.

4. After you have picked up the litter, you can sort it. Separate recyclables such as bottles, cans, paper, and plastics (see Figure 13). Many of the cans and bottles can be redeemed for money. The money may be shared among squad members or donated to your school or a favorite charity. Other nonrecyclable litter might include such things as yard waste, cigarette butts, scrap paper, and food waste.

5. Keep a record of the types of litter you collect. If you plan to use your activity as a science fair project, you should weigh each type of litter. That data can be used to prepare bar graphs for display.

6. You might take the trash to your local landfill director. Do the percentages of different types of litter that you collected agree with those found at the landfill? Does the landfill provide bins for recyclables? If not, you might suggest to local officials that they be added.

7. Have the litter removal squad or squads discuss the sources of the litter. Then talk about what can be done to reduce or eliminate it.

8. Make what you have done known to your school, your community, and a local newspaper. Your actions may inspire others to think before they litter.

9. Your town or city probably has laws that prohibit littering. Alert the police about where you found litter and what you think its source is. It could be a person or persons, or it could be from a trash collecting truck that failed to cover the trash in transit. What might be other sources of the litter? Perhaps signs reading PLEASE DON'T LITTER or RECYCLE YES, LITTER NO will help.

5.2 Beachcombing for Litter
(An Activity)

Things YOU will Need:
- ✓ work gloves
- ✓ garbage bags
- ✓ pen or pencil
- ✓ notebook

If you live near an ocean, you can beachcomb for litter while enjoying sea breezes, salt air, sandy beaches, and the beautiful sea. Unfortunately, inconsiderate people often leave litter on the beach. And the tides, wind, and waves often bring additional litter from afar.

You can beachcomb alone or with friends, classmates, or family. Just be sure to get your parents' permission first.

1. As you start beachcombing for litter, be sure to wear work gloves and carry a garbage bag to hold the litter you find. Place recyclable items in a second bag.

2. Even with gloves, be careful when you pick up sharp objects. Do not pick up anything that looks like a syringe needle. **Ask an adult for help.**

3. Keep a record of what you find. Which parts of the litter do you think were left by beachgoers? Which do you think washed up from the sea? What makes you think so?

People often leave litter on the beach when they visit, and litter also washes up from the ocean.

4. If there are local organizations that try to keep the beaches clean, you could join the group. If not, try to organize people who will help you beachcomb for litter and recyclables. Your local newspaper or community website will probably be happy to publish your request for volunteers.

Plastics and Animals

Some of the litter you may have found on a beach is the same kind of litter that causes the death of marine animals. About 100,000 sea mammals and 2 million seabirds are killed every year by plastic littering the seas.

Plastic six-pack rings are often found around the necks of dead birds. Simply cutting the rings before discarding them can prevent them from ever encircling an animal's neck or limbs. Seabirds often eat plastic pieces because they view them as food. Sea turtles swallow plastic bags; they mistake them for jellyfish. Dissection of one beached whale revealed 50 plastic bags in the mammal's stomach. Such plastics may block an animal's digestive tract, causing it to starve to death. Many sea animals become entangled in abandoned fishing nets and lines.

5.3 Simulating Entanglement
(A Demonstration)

Things YOU will Need:

☑ a partner
☑ large rubber band

Animals often become entangled by litter and are unable to escape.

1. To see how this can happen, have someone wrap a rubber band around your hand as shown in Figure 14.

2. Try to remove the rubber band without using your other hand. Remember, most animals do not have hands. Not easy, is it!

3. Be sure to remove the rubber band before your skin turns blue.

Precycling

Precycling involves thinking before buying. Is the product you plan to buy surrounded by a large amount of plastic or paper packaging that you will have to discard? If it is, consider buying larger amounts with less packaging per weight. Instead of small juice boxes that can't be recycled, buy frozen juice in a can. Mix the frozen juice with water at home and carry it in a thermos bottle. Or buy large recyclable bottles of juice and store them in your refrigerator.

Can the plastic containers that hold items you plan to buy be recycled or used again? Can you make your own cleaning product from common chemicals such as baking soda and vinegar rather than buying a commercial brand in a container that can't be recycled?

What about plastic clothes hangers? At some stores you can buy hangers made of corn or bamboo. Most dry cleaners will gladly accept metal hangers you might be planning to discard.

Figure 14

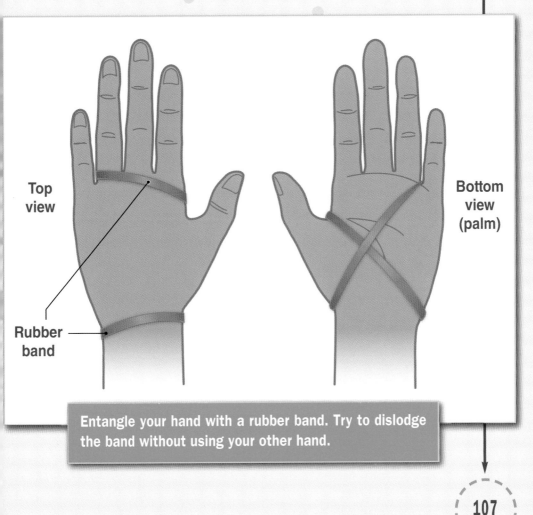

Top view

Bottom view (palm)

Rubber band

Entangle your hand with a rubber band. Try to dislodge the band without using your other hand.

Source Reduction

Manufacturers are helping to lessen solid waste by reducing the weight of the source used to make their product. As a result, glass bottles weigh about half as much as they did in the 1970s. Plastic bottles are also lighter, though not by as significant an amount as glass. Steel cans are lighter and are coated with a thinner layer of the tin that prevents rusting. Since 1970, the weight of aluminum cans has nearly halved. Even cardboard boxes have become lighter and newspapers have reduced the thickness of their pages. The number of pages has also been reduced, but part of this reduction is the result of a decline in readership as more people obtain their news electronically.

5.4 Precycling: Consider the Packaging Before You Buy (An Analysis)

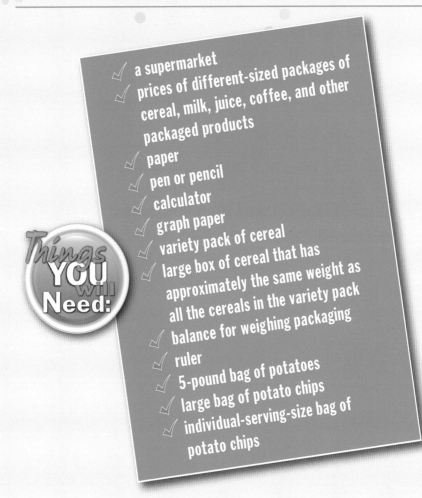

- a supermarket
- prices of different-sized packages of cereal, milk, juice, coffee, and other packaged products
- paper
- pen or pencil
- calculator
- graph paper
- variety pack of cereal
- large box of cereal that has approximately the same weight as all the cereals in the variety pack
- balance for weighing packaging
- ruler
- 5-pound bag of potatoes
- large bag of potato chips
- individual-serving-size bag of potato chips

$\mathbf{Y}$our great-grandparents probably lived in an area that was primarily rural. They grew their own food or bought it from nearby farms. To prepare for winter, food was stored in a cellar or was salted, smoked, or canned. Today, we live in a predominantly urban nation. Our food is grown in various parts of the world. Much of it comes in packages. Packaging increases the price of the food and adds to the solid waste we discard.

How does the price of a 12-ounce box of cereal compare with the price of a 24-ounce box of the same cereal? Is it half the price of the larger box?

To see how price is related to packaging and size, you can do an analysis.

1. At a supermarket, compare the prices of different-sized packages of cereal, milk, juice, coffee, and other packaged products. For each product of a certain brand, record its name, the size of the package, and its price. When you get home, you can calculate the price per unit weight or volume and make a chart for each food you examined. A sample chart is shown below.

| Item | Brand | Size | Price | Price Per | |
				Pound	Ounce
bran flakes	X	24 oz.	$5.35	$3.57	$0.22
bran flakes	X	18 oz.	$4.50	$4.00	$0.25
bran flakes	X	12 oz.	$3.25	$4.33	$0.27

2. For each product you examined, plot a graph of price per ounce versus package size. A sample graph for the data in the chart above is shown in Figure 15.

    As the package size decreases, what happens to the price per pound or ounce? Can you explain why?

Figure 15

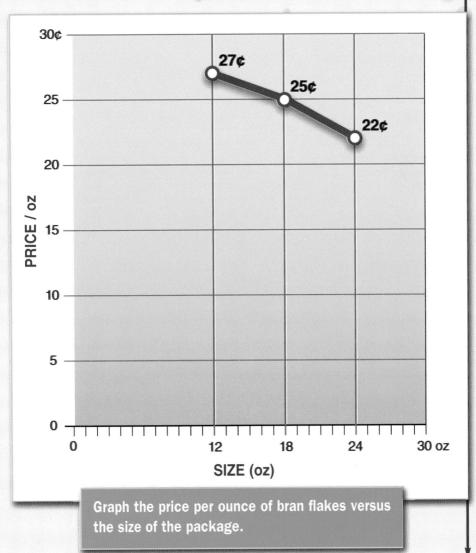

Graph the price per ounce of bran flakes versus the size of the package.

3. With permission, buy a variety pack of cereal, one that has 10 or 12 single servings of cereal. At the same time, buy a large box of cereal that has approximately the same weight as all the cereals in the variety pack. Keep all the packaging as the cereals are eaten.

4. When all the cereals are gone, weigh all the packaging that contained and surrounded the variety pack. Then weigh the packaging that surrounded the cereal in the large box. How do the two weights compare?

5. Measure the area, in square centimeters or square inches, of all the packaging that was in the variety pack. Then do the same thing for the large box of cereal. How do these areas compare? How is area related to the amount of packaging?

6. Processing, as well as packaging, affects the price of a product. Find and record the price of a 5-pound bag of potatoes, a large bag of potato chips (you will find the weight somewhere on the bag), and a small individual-serving-size bag of potato chips. Calculate the price per pound for each. How do they compare? Can you explain why?

Idea for a Science Fair Project

- Investigate what factors companies consider when they design packages to hold food and other products. Do you think shape is one? How about color? Pictures or photographs? Print size and font?

RecycleBank

RecycleBank is a company that strives to turn trash into money for those who buy into it. The idea is to offer a financial incentive for recycling. RecycleBank participants use 96-gallon containers that sport a piggy bank and garbage can logo. All recyclables—cans, paper, plastics, glass—go into the container. It is called "single stream" recycling. It encourages recycling because users do not have to separate recyclables. Trucks that pick up the large containers weigh each one before emptying it. Radio-frequency ID tags embedded in the containers are scanned. The weight data is transmitted to a website and converted into points. Households receive 2.5 points for every pound of recyclables. Each point is worth 10 cents and can be redeemed at participating stores such as CVS, Starbucks, or national brands such as Coca-Cola.

RecycleBank makes its money by charging retail partners for online advertising and from cities that save money by reducing the volume of trash sent to landfills and waste-to-energy plants.

A Greener Halloween

Planning a Halloween party? Make it green. Don't waste paper on invitations. Use e-mails.

Need a costume? The store-bought kind will probably come in excessive packaging, and they are often made with petroleum products imported from other countries. Why not search your closet or visit a thrift shop? You can probably find something suitable and ghoulish for next to nothing.

You can have a "green" Halloween by making your own costume. This robot was made out of cardboard boxes and paint.

5.5 Find Out About Recycling in Your Town or City (An Activity)

Things YOU will Need:
- ✓ telephone or computer with Internet connection (optional)
- ✓ notebook
- ✓ pen or pencil

If a recycling program is available in your town or city, is there a curbside pickup service? Or do citizens have to take recyclables to a recycling center or transfer station? If there is curbside pickup, are there separate trucks for recyclables and for other trash? Or does the same truck pick up both recyclables and trash to throw away?

If there is curbside pickup, do you have to separate glass, plastic, paper, and cans from other solid waste? Or can all recyclables be placed in the same container? Are plastics recycled? If so, are only certain plastics, such as numbers 1 and 2 accepted for recycling?

If there is no recycling program in your community, talk to local officials about the possibility of starting such a program.

5.6 Recycling at School (An Activity)

Things YOU will Need:

✓ trash cans, bins, or other receptacles for recyclables and other waste

✓ materials to make signs (posterboard and markers, for example)

Does your school have a recycling program? If not, talk to your principal about establishing one.

1. Talk to a local public works official or your librarian. Find out what waste can be recycled. Not everything is recyclable. For instance, unlike bottles and cans, cardboard milk and juice cartons can't be recycled. They have a plastic lining that is difficult to separate from the cardboard. Juice boxes have closely bonded layers of plastic, paper, and aluminum foil that make them nonrecyclable.

2. If your community recycles and your principal offers support, start a recycling program in your school.

3. Most waste is probably created in your school's cafeteria. You, or a recycling committee you organize, can provide trash cans, bins, or other receptacles for recyclables and other waste.

4. Place signs on or above these containers so that people know where to drop recyclables and other trash. Signs might read CANS, GLASS BOTTLES, PLASTIC BOTTLES, PAPER, and OTHER TRASH.

5. Arrange to have the recyclables picked up if your town has this service. If not, find a way to transport them to a recycling center.

6. If bottles and cans can be redeemed for 5¢ or 10¢ each, encourage students and teachers to return these items for money. If they would rather discard them, it's your chance to make some money for the school or for yourself.

5.7 Recycling in the Classroom
(An Experiment)

What kinds of waste would you expect to find in a classroom? Form a hypothesis. Then do this experiment. Ask your teacher for permission before you begin.

1. Near the end of a school day, examine the wastebasket or other waste receptacle where students and teachers discard items in your classroom or classrooms.

2. Put on plastic or rubber gloves before you separate and classify the contents. Record the various contents you find. Record, too, the weight of each kind of waste.

3. Assuming this is an average day, calculate the weight of trash that would be discarded in a week, a month, and an entire school year.

4. What can you do to see if your one-day weighing is a daily average?

5. What can you do to estimate the total weight of trash generated in your school each day?

6. Report your results to your teacher or classmates and offer recommendations. For example, if you find that most paper has writing on only one side, you might suggest that people use both sides of a piece of paper before discarding it. Point out that discarded paper clips or thumbtacks could be reused rather than discarded. Provide containers where such items can be deposited. Cans, bottles, paper, and other recyclables should be recycled and not discarded.

5.8 A Zero-Waste Lunch (An Activity)

Things YOU will Need:
- ✓ lunch taken to school

1. If you take your lunch to school, record the items that you discard as waste after eating your lunch.

2. Challenge yourself or whoever packs your lunch to pack a zero-waste lunch. Then check to see if you throw anything away after eating that lunch.

3. Challenge your classmates to bring zero-waste lunches to school.

4. Challenge the entire school to bring zero-waste lunches. Perhaps this would be a good idea for Earth Day.

5. If your school has a cafeteria, talk to the cafeteria director about preparing zero-waste meals.

5.8 Which Cup Should I Buy for One-Time Use? (An Experiment)

Things YOU will Need:
- ✓ foam cup
- ✓ paper cup
- ✓ balance for weighing (± 0.1 g)
- ✓ metric ruler

Should you buy paper cups or polystyrene foam (#6 PS) cups for one-time use? Form a hypothesis. Then do this experiment.

By this point in the book, you would probably say, "I would not buy either. I would use glass cups or drinking glasses, or biodegradable products."

That is the best answer; however, pretend this is for a big party and you don't have enough glassware. You are forced to buy paper or plastic.

1. Examine a foam cup and a paper cup carefully (see Figure 16). What materials are found in each cup?

   Examine the paper cup carefully. It may be made of more than just paper. Which cup would be easier to recycle?

2. Weigh each cup. Record the mass of each cup in grams.

3. Step on each cup. Crush it into as small a volume as possible.

4. Use a ruler and your math knowledge to calculate the volume occupied by each crushed cup. Which cup

would take up the least space in a landfill? Is either cup biodegradable?

5. It takes 2.8 times more energy to manufacture a gram of plastic than to make a gram of paper. Which required more energy to make, the paper or the plastic?

6. Recycling plastic saves 4.1 times more energy per gram than does recycling paper.

   Which cup will save more energy if recycled?

7. When burned in a waste-to-energy plant, plastic produces 2.8 times more heat per gram than does paper. Which cup will generate more heat if burned?

8. Based on all the information, which cup will you buy? Why?

Figure 16

Which cup should you buy?

Glossary

alloy—A mixture of two or more metals.

aluminum—A lightweight metal that, when used in an alloy, is strong and hard.

bacteria—Single-celled organisms that can decompose organic matter. Some bacteria can cause disease.

biodegradable—Able to be decomposed in nature.

blast furnace—A furnace used to smelt ore.

carbon—An element present in organic (living or previously living) matter. It is used to make steel, an alloy of iron.

composting—Using microorganisms to decompose waste into useful soil.

copper—A metal that is an excellent conductor of heat and electricity.

curbside—Between the sidewalk and the street; along the curb.

deposit—A charge added to the cost of an item, such as a bottle or can, and given back when the item is returned to the seller for recycling or reuse.

fossil fuel—A resource that can be burned for fuel and that is made from the fossilized remains of ancient plants or animals, such as coal, oil, or natural gas.

groundwater—Water found beneath the ground.

incinerate—To burn to ashes, often to produce steam to generate electricity.

iron—A metal that rusts and is attracted to magnets. It is commonly made into steel.

landfill—A place where solid waste is buried in soil.

leachate—Liquid that has percolated through soil, such as the soil in a landfill, dissolving some substances as it goes. The substances in the leachate may pollute groundwater.

lead—A heavy metal used for electrodes in lead storage batteries.

mercury—A heavy, liquid metal used in small batteries, fluorescent lights, and various scientific instruments.

microorganisms—Living organisms, such as fungi and bacteria, that are so small they can be seen only with the aid of a microscope. Such organisms are vital in the decomposition of organic matter.

nonrenewables—Resources, such as fossil fuels, that cannot be replaced because they are available only in limited amounts.

ore—A rock that contains a metal that can be separated by smelting.

pig iron—Iron that comes from a blast furnace. In addition to iron, it contains about 4 percent carbon, 2 percent silicon, 1 percent phosphorus, and traces of sulfur.

recyclable—Able to be reprocessed for reuse.

recycling—Collecting and reprocessing products such as cans, paper, and bottles so that their components can be reused.

renewable—A resource such as sunlight, wind, and water that can be replaced quickly.

scrubbers—Devices used to remove or clean emissions before they are released into the atmosphere.

smelting—Separating a metal from its ore by heating the ore to a high temperature.

solid waste—Solid materials that are discarded, such as trash, food waste, ashes, furniture, appliances, and electronics.

steel—A strong, flexible alloy of iron.

tin—A soft metal; it is used to coat steel cans to prevent them from rusting.

toxic—Poisonous.

Appendix:
Science Supply Companies

Arbor Scientific
P.O. Box 2750
Ann Arbor, MI 48106-2750
(800) 367-6695
www.arborsci.com

Carolina Biological Supply Co.
2700 York Road
Burlington, NC 27215-3398
(800) 334-5551
http://www.carolina.com

Connecticut Valley Biological Supply Co., Inc.
82 Valley Road, Box 326
Southampton, MA 01073
(800) 628-7748
http://www.ctvalleybio.com

Delta Education
P.O. Box 3000
80 Northwest Blvd
Nashua, NH 03061-3000
(800) 258-1302
customerservice@delta-
    education.com

Edmund Scientific's Scientifics
60 Pearce Avenue
Tonawanda, NY 14150-6711
(800) 728-6999
http://www.scientificsonline.com

Educational Innovations, Inc.
362 Main Avenue
Norwalk, CT 06851
(888) 912-7474
http://www.teachersource.com

Fisher Science Education
4500 Turnberry
Hanover Park, IL 60133
(800) 955-1177
http://www.fisheredu.com

Frey Scientific
100 Paragon Parkway
Mansfield, OH 44903
(800) 225-3739
http://www.freyscientific.com

Nasco-Fort Atkinson
P.O. Box 901
Fort Atkinson, WI 53538-0901
(800) 558-9595
http://www.enasco.com

Nasco-Modesto
P.O. Box 3837
Modesto, CA 95352-3837
(800) 558-9595
http://www.enasco.com

Sargent-Welch/VWR Scientific
P.O. Box 5229
Buffalo Grove, IL 60089-5229
(800) SAR-GENT
http://www.SargentWelch.com

Science Kit & Boreal Laboratories
777 East Park Drive
P.O. Box 5003
Tonawanda, NY 14150
(800) 828-7777
http://sciencekit.com

Wards Natural Science Establishment
P.O. Box 92912
Rochester, NY 14692-9012
(800) 962-2660
http://www.wardsci.com

Further Reading

Books

Bardhan-Quallen, Sudipta. *Championship Science Fair Projects: 100 Sure-to-Win Experiments.* New York: Sterling, 2005.

David, Sarah B. *Reducing Your Carbon Footprint at Home.* New York: The Rosen Publishing Group, Inc., 2009.

Jefferis, David. *Green Power: Eco-energy without Pollution.* New York: Crabtree Publishing Company, 2006.

McKay, Kim, and Jenny Bonnin. *True Green Kids: 100 Things You Can Do to Save the Planet.* Washington, DC: National Geographic Society, 2008.

Parks, Peggy J. *Global Warming.* San Diego: Kidhaven Press, 2005.

Rhadigan, Joe, and Rain Newcomb. *Prize-Winning Science Fair Projects for Curious Kids.* New York: Lark Books, 2004.

Sobha, Geeta. *Green Technology: Earth-Friendly Innovations.* New York: Crabtree Publishing Company, 2008.

Woodward, John. *Climate Change.* New York: DK Publishing, 2008.

Internet Addresses

Act Green
http://www.scholastic.com/actgreen/

Recycling 101
www.earth911.org/recycling/

Recycling Revolution
www.recycling-revolution.com

Index

A

aluminum recycling, 74, 76–84, 108
amperes, 54
Appert, Nicolas, 77

B

batteries, 78
bauxite, 76
bottled water, 70
browns, 59
butene, 13–14

C

cans, separating, 80–84
classroom recycling, 118–119
Clean Air Act of 1970, 33
clothes hangers, 107
composting, 57–62
cups, single-use, 121–122

D

decomposition
    composting, 57–62
    observing, 44, 47–49
    in soil, 41–43
    water and, 45
density measurement, 21–28
diapers, polymers in, 15–17
dilutions, making, 65–69
Durand, Peter, 77

E

earthworms in composting, 61–62
electricity generation demonstration,
    53–55
electromagnets, 50, 83–84, 96
energy conservation in recycling, 17,
    34
entanglement simulation, 106, 107
ethylene, 13–14
e-waste, 86
experiments, designing, 8–9

F

five Rs, 49
food safety history, 77

G

gasohol, 52
glass, 77, 85–88, 108
green Halloween, 114
greens, 59
greenwashing, 72

H

Halloween, 114
HDPE (high-density polyethylene), 18,
    20, 26
how you can help, 69–71, 99
    beachcombing for litter, 103–104
    glass, 87–88
    green Halloween, 114
    litter removal squad, 100–102
    paper recycling, 88–90
    precycling, 106–107, 109–112
    recycling program research, 115
    school recycling, 116–120
    source reduction, 108

I

iron (steel) recycling, 74–76, 79–84,
    108

L

landfills
    decomposition in, 41–45
    history of, 33–34
    indestructible bulk in, 14
    leaching prevention model, 38–40
    pollution modeling, 35–37
LDPE (low-density polyethylene), 18,
    19, 26
lead, 78

M

maggots, 48
mercury, 11, 78
metals recycling, 50, 74–79
moth repellents, 71

N

nonrenewable sources, 98
North Pacific Garbage Patch (Pacific Trash Vortex), 31

P

packaging, price and, 109–112
paper
    fibers, viewing, 91
    making, process of, 86–90
    recycling, 34, 49, 69–70, 86–90, 92–94
    source reduction, 108
"pay as you throw" (PAYT) approach, 40
PET (polyethylene terephthalate), 17, 18, 20, 25
plastic bags, 70, 71, 105
plastics, 12–14
    animals and, 105–107
    burning, 29–30
    density of, 21–24
    identification by density, 25–28
    recycling, 17
    types of, 17–20
polluting substances measurement, 65–69
polyethylene, 18, 19, 26
polymerization, 13–14
polymers, 13–17
PP (polypropylene), 18, 19, 20, 26
precycling, 106–107, 109–112
PS (polystyrene), 18, 19, 20, 26
pulping, 89
PVC (polyvinyl chloride), 18, 26

R

RecycleBank, 113
recycling program research, 115
Redi, Francesco, 47–49
refuse-derived fuel, 50
renewable sources, 97

S

safety, 11
school recycling, 116–120
science fairs, 10
scientific method, 8–9
single-stream recycling, 113
sizing, 89
solid waste
    biodegradable, 41–45
    disposal of historically, 32–34
    green processing of, 50–52
    natural resources trapped in, 97–98
    ocean dumping of, 31
    source reduction, 108
    trash, separating, 95–96, 102
spontaneous generation, 47–49
spores, 48
steel (iron) recycling, 74–76, 79–84, 108
surface area and volume, 60, 63–64, 73

T

thermometers, 11, 78
trash, separating, 95–96, 102

V

variables, 8–9

W

waste-to-energy plants, 50–55
weight of water absorbed per gram of polymer ratio, 16
Wohler, Freidrich, 12

Z

zero-waste lunch, 120